Steven I. Pfeiffer, PhD
Linda A. Reddy, PhD
Editors

Innovative Mental Health Interventions for Children: Programs That Work

Innovative Mental Health Interventions for Children: Programs That Work has been co-published simultaneously as *Residential Treatment for Children & Youth,* Volume 18, Number 3 2001.

Pre-publication
REVIEWS,
COMMENTARIES,
EVALUATIONS . . .

"**A**N EXTREMELY VALUABLE RE-SOURCE FOR PSYCHOLOGISTS AND OTHER MENTAL HEALTH PROFESSIONALS. Clear and concise . . . strong emphasis on validation. I would recommend this book to anyone wishing to expand his/her role in treating children or anyone who now treats those with typical childhood problems but would like to do better."

David L. Wodrich, PhD, ABPP
Department of Psychology
Phoenix Children's Hospital
Clinical Associate Professor of Pediatrics
The University of Arizona
Health Sciences Center

More pre-publication
REVIEWS, COMMENTARIES, EVALUATIONS . . .

"**I** commend the authors for commissioning this collection of innovative intervention programs. THEY HAVE DONE A TREMENDOUS FAVOR FOR OUR FIELD . . . should be read by anyone committed to providing services for this difficult and vulnerable population. IT CAN BE EXTREMELY GRATIFYING TO BE AN AGENT OF POSITIVE CHANGE!"

Marilyn B. Benoit, MD, FAACAP
President-Elect
American Academy of Child
and Adolescent Psychiatry
Associate Clinical Professor
of Psychiatry
Georgetown University Medical Center
Washington, DC

The Haworth Press, Inc.

Innovative Mental Health Interventions for Children: Programs That Work

Innovative Mental Health Interventions for Children: Programs That Work has been co-published simultaneously as *Residential Treatment for Children & Youth,* Volume 18, Number 3 2001.

The *Residential Treatment for Children & Youth* Monographic "Separates"

Below is a list of "separates," which in serials librarianship means a special issue simultaneously published as a special journal issue or double-issue *and* as a "separate" hardbound monograph. (This is a format which we also call a "DocuSerial.")

"Separates" are published because specialized libraries or professionals may wish to purchase a specific thematic issue by itself in a format which can be separately cataloged and shelved, as opposed to purchasing the journal on an on-going basis. Faculty members may also more easily consider a "separate" for classroom adoption.

"Separates" are carefully classified separately with the major book jobbers so that the journal tie-in can be noted on new book order slips to avoid duplicate purchasing.

You may wish to visit Haworth's website at . . .

http://www.HaworthPress.com

. . . to search our online catalog for complete tables of contents of these separates and related publications.

You may also call 1-800-HAWORTH (outside US/Canada: 607-722-5857), or Fax: 1-800-895-0582 (outside US/Canada: 607-771-0012), or e-mail at:

getinfo@haworthpressinc.com

Innovative Mental Health Interventions for Children: Programs That Work, edited by Steven I. Pfeiffer, PhD, and Linda A. Reddy, PhD (Vol. 18, No. 3, 2001). *"AN EXTREMELY VALUABLE RESOURCE FOR PSYCHOLOGISTS AND OTHER MENTAL HEALTH PROFESSIONALS. Clear and concise . . . strong emphasis on validation. I would recommend this book to anyone wishing to expand his/her role in treating children or anyone who now treats those with typical childhood problems but would like to do better." (David L. Wodrich, PhD, ABPP, Department of Psychology, Phoenix Children's Hospital; Clinical Associate Professor of Pediatrics, The University of Arizona Health Sciences Center)*

The Forsaken Child: Essays on Group Care and Individual Therapy, by D. Patrick Zimmerman, PsyD (Vol. 18, No. 2, 2000). *"A MUST READ for anyone concerned about the quality of care of disturbed children and youth. Zimmerman is truly the 'great chronicler' and the 'keeper of the flame' of quality group care." (Robert B. Bloom, PhD, Executive Director, Jewish Children's Bureau, Chicago, Illinois)*

Family-Centered Services in Residential Treatment: New Approaches for Group Care, edited by John Y. Powell, PhD (Vol. 17, No. 3, 2000). *"Offers suggestions and methods for incorporating parents and youths into successful treatment programs in temporary and long-term settings. This essential guide will help psychologists, therapists, and social workers unite theory and practice to create a family-oriented environment for troubled clients and provide effective services. Containing case studies, personal discoveries, and insights about the potentials and limitations of residential care, this reliable resource will help you develop improved services for youths with the help of their families using reevaluated techniques to meet individual needs."*

The New Board: Changing Issues, Roles and Relationships, edited by Nadia Ehrlich Finkelstein, MS, ACSW, and Raymond Schimmer, MAT (Vol. 16, No. 4, 1999). *This innovative book offers very specific, real life examples and informed recommendations for board management of nonprofit residential service agencies and explains why and how to consider redesigning your board form and practice. You will explore variations of board structures, managed care pressure, increased complexity of service, reduced board member availability, and relevant theoretical discussions complete with pertinent reports on the practice of boards in the nonprofit residential service field.*

Outcome Assessment in Residential Treatment, edited by Steven I. Pfeiffer, PhD (Vol. 13, No. 4, 1996). *"Presents a logical and systematic response, based on research, to the detractors of residential treatment centers." (Canada's Children (Child Welfare League of Canada))*

Residential Education as an Option for At-Risk Youth, edited by Jerome Beker, EdD, and Douglas Magnuson, MA (Vol. 13, No. 3, 1996). *"As a remarkable leap forward, as an approach to child welfare, it is required reading for professionals–from child care workers to administrators and planners–or for anyone in search of hope for children trapped in the bitter problems of a blighted and disordered existence . . . It is instructive, practical, and humanistic."* (Howard Goldstein, DSW, Professor Emeritus, Case Western Reserve University; Author, The Home on Gorham Street)

When Love Is Not Enough: The Management of Covert Dynamics in Organizations that Treat Children and Adolescents, edited by Donna Piazza, PhD (Vol. 13, No. 1, 1996). *"Addresses the difficult question of 'unconscious dynamics' within institutions which care for children and adolescents. The subject matter makes for fascinating reading, and anyone who has had experience of residential institutions for disturbed children will find themselves nodding in agreement throughout the book."* (Emotional and Behavioural Difficulties)

Applied Research in Residential Treatment, edited by Gordon Northrup, MD (Vol. 12, No. 1, 1995). *"The authors suggest appropriate topics for research projects, give practical suggestions on design, and provide example research reports."* (Reference & Research Book News)

Managing the Residential Treatment Center in Troubled Times, edited by Gordon Northrup, MD (Vol. 11, No. 4, 1994). *"A challenging manual for a challenging decade. . . .Takes the eminently sensible position that our failures are as worthy of analysis as our successes. This approach is both sobering and instructive."* (Nancy Woodruff Ment, MSW, BCD, Associate Executive Director, Julia Dyckman Andrus Memorial, Yonkers, New York)

The Management of Sexuality in Residential Treatment, edited by Gordon Northrup, MD (Vol. 11, No. 2, 1994). *"Must reading for residential treatment center administrators and all treatment personnel."* (Irving N. Berlin, MD, Emeritus Professor, School of Medicine, University of New Mexico; Clinical Director, Child & Adolescent Services, Charter Hospital of Albuquerque and Medical Director, Namaste Residential Treatment Center)

Sexual Abuse and Residential Treatment, edited by Wander de C. Braga, MD, and Raymond Schimmer (Vol. 11, No. 1, 1994). *"Ideas are presented for assisting victims in dealing with past abuse and protecting them from future abuse in the facility."* (Coalition Commentary (Illinois Coalition Against Sexual Assault))

Milieu Therapy: Significant Issues and Innovative Applications, edited by Jerome M. Goldsmith, EdD, and Jacquelyn Sanders, PhD (Vol. 10, No. 3, 1993). *This tribute to Bruno Bettelheim illuminates continuing efforts to further understanding of the caring process and its impact upon healing and repair measures for disturbed children in residential care.*

Severely Disturbed Youngsters and the Parental Alliance, edited by Jacquelyn Sanders, PhD, and Barry L. Childress, MD (Vol. 9, No. 4, 1992). *"Establishes the importance of a therapeutic alliance with the parents of severely disturbed young people to improve the success of counseling."* (Public Welfare)

Crisis Intervention in Residential Treatment: The Clinical Innovations of Fritz Redl, edited by William C. Morse, PhD (Vol. 8, No. 4, 1991). *"Valuable in helping us set directions for continuing Redl's courageous trail-blazing work."* (Reading (A Journal of Reviews and Commentary in Mental Health))

Adolescent Suicide: Recognition, Treatment and Prevention, edited by Barry Garfinkel, MD, and Gordon Northrup, MD (Vol. 7, No. 1, 1990). *"Distills highly relevant information about the identification and treatment of suicidal adolescents into a pithy volume which will be highly accessible by all mental health professionals."* (Norman E. Alessi, MD, Director, Child Diagnostic and Research Unit, The University of Michigan Medical Center)

Psychoanalytic Approaches to the Very Troubled Child: Therapeutic Practice Innovations in Residential and Educational Settings, edited by Jacquelyn Sanders, PhD, and Barry M. Childress, MD (Vol. 6, No. 4, 1989). *"I find myself wanting to re-read the book–which I recommend for every professional library shelf, especially for directors of programs dealing with the management of residentially located disturbed youth."* (Journal of American Association of Psychiatric Administrators)

Innovative Mental Health Interventions for Children: Programs That Work

Steven I. Pfeiffer, PhD
Linda A. Reddy, PhD
Editors

Innovative Mental Health Interventions for Children: Programs That Work has been co-published simultaneously as *Residential Treatment for Children & Youth,* Volume 18, Number 3 2001.

The Haworth Press, Inc.
New York • London • Oxford

Innovative Mental Health Interventions for Children: Programs That Work has been co-published simultaneously as *Residential Treatment for Children & Youth* ™, Volume 18, Number 3 2001.

The development, preparation, and publication of this work has been undertaken with great care. However, the publisher, employees, editors, and agents of The Haworth Press and all imprints of The Haworth Press, Inc., including The Haworth Medical Press® and Pharmaceutical Products Press®, are not responsible for any errors contained herein or for consequences that may ensue from use of materials or information contained in this work. Opinions expressed by the author(s) are not necessarily those of The Haworth Press, Inc.

Cover design by Thomas J. Mayshock Jr.

Library of Congress Cataloging-in-Publication Data

Innovative mental health interventions for children : programs that work / Steven I. Pfeiffer, Linda A. Reddy, editors.
      p. cm.
    Includes bibliographical references and index.
    ISBN 0-7890-1363-0 (alk. paper)–ISBN 0-7890-1364-9 (alk. paper)
    1. Child mental health services. 2. Child mental health services–United States. 3. Child psychotherapy. 4. Mental illness–Prevention. I. Pfeiffer, Steven I. II. Reddy, Linda A. III. Residential treatment for children & youth.
RJ499 .I54 2001
362.2′083–dc21
                                               2001024318

Indexing, Abstracting & Website/Internet Coverage

This section provides you with a list of major indexing & abstracting services. That is to say, each service began covering this periodical during the year noted in the right column. Most Websites which are listed below have indicated that they will either post, disseminate, compile, archive, cite or alert their own Website users with research-based content from this work. (This list is as current as the copyright date of this publication.)

(continued)

Special Bibliographic Notes related to special journal issues (separates) and indexing/abstracting:

- indexing/abstracting services in this list will also cover material in any "separate" that is co-published simultaneously with Haworth's special thematic journal issue or DocuSerial. Indexing/abstracting usually covers material at the article/chapter level.
- monographic co-editions are intended for either non-subscribers or libraries which intend to purchase a second copy for their circulating collections.
- monographic co-editions are reported to all jobbers/wholesalers/approval plans. The source journal is listed as the "series" to assist the prevention of duplicate purchasing in the same manner utilized for books-in-series.
- to facilitate user/access services all indexing/abstracting services are encouraged to utilize the co-indexing entry note indicated at the bottom of the first page of each article/chapter/contribution.
- this is intended to assist a library user of any reference tool (whether print, electronic, online, or CD-ROM) to locate the monographic version if the library has purchased this version but not a subscription to the source journal.
- individual articles/chapters in any Haworth publication are also available through the Haworth Document Delivery Service (HDDS).

Innovative Mental Health Interventions for Children: Programs That Work

CONTENTS

ABOUT THE EDITORS

Steven I. Pfeiffer, PhD, received his PhD from the University of North Carolina-Chapel Hill in 1977. He is Executive Director of the Duke Talent Identification Program and Adjunct Professor of Psychology at Duke University, Durham, North Carolina. Dr. Pfeiffer is a Fellow of APA, a diplomate of the American Board of Professional Psychology, and is listed in the National Register of Health Service Providers in Psychology.

Author of more than one hundred articles and book chapters, and co-author of the Devereux Behavior Rating Scales, Dr. Pfeiffer has served as Editor in Chief of the journal of *Child and Adolescent Mental Health Care*, was Guest Editor of *Outcome Assessment in Residential Treatment* (Haworth), and is on the editorial boards of six professional journals. His present interests are prevention and early intervention with high risk youth, programs for the gifted, and the psychology of sports.

Linda A. Reddy, PhD, received her doctorate in School Psychology from the University of Arizona in 1994 and completed a two-year Postdoctoral Fellowship at the Devereux Foundation Institute of Clinical Training and Research. Dr. Reddy is Assistant Professor and Director of the Child and Adolescent ADHD Clinic at Fairleigh Dickinson University. Dr. Reddy is also Research Associate at the Devereux Foundation Institute of Clinical Training and Research. Her research interests include family and school interventions, child behavior disorders, assessment, consultation, and treatment outcome evaluation.

Preface

In the chapter entitled I Can Problem Solve (ICPS), Myrna B. Shure describes an interpersonal cognitive problem solving program which is aimed at reducing and preventing high risk behaviors in young children. These behaviors such as aggression, poor peer relationships, low frustration tolerance and social withdrawal in children can lead to significant adolescent behavior problems, for example, violence, substance abuse, and school failure. ICPS enables children as young as 4 years old to develop a problem solving thinking style to cope with stressful situations. The program is designed for use in the school setting with implementation by the child's school teacher. There is also a supplemental program for parents to assist their children with cognitive problem solving. ICPS has been shown to be beneficial for children from diverse ethnic backgrounds and socioeconomic classes. Specifically, impulsivity and behavioral inhibition have been reduced following children's participation in the program.

A video-based program designed to reduce substance abuse and behavioral problems in young adolescents, the Strengthening Families Program for Young Adolescents, is described in the chapter by Virginia Molgaard and Richard Spoth. This program views the family as having significant influence on young adolescents' behaviors, in terms of family liabilities (e.g., family conflict) and strengths (e.g., coping skills). Individual and conjoint sessions for parents and their adolescents are conducted by group leaders. Major objectives of the sessions are to increase appropriate interaction and communication between parents and adolescents as well as to identify family values. The program is designed for all socioeconomic and ethnic groups. Outcome research has demonstrated

---

[Haworth co-indexing entry note]: "Preface." Dineen-Wagner, Karen. Co-published simultaneously in *Residential Treatment for Children & Youth* (The Haworth Press, Inc.) Vol. 18, No. 3, 2001, pp. xix-xxii; and: *Innovative Mental Health Interventions for Children: Programs That Work* (ed: Steven I. Pfeiffer, and Linda A. Reddy) The Haworth Press, Inc., 2001, pp. xiii-xvi. Single or multiple copies of this article are available for a fee from The Haworth Document Delivery Service [1-800-342-9678, 9:00 a.m. - 5:00 p.m. (EST). E-mail address: getinfo@haworthpressinc.com].

that parents and adolescents who have participated in this program have an increased level of positive interaction. Moreover, adolescent participants have less substance abuse, antisocial behaviors and school behavioral problems compared to adolescents who were not in the program.

The importance of a positive family environment is also emphasized in the Teaching-Family Model (TMF) described by Kathryn A. Kirigin. This program is designed for children and adolescents with emotional and behavioral problems in residential treatment centers. Learning theory underlies the TFM in that problem behaviors are viewed as a product of stressful daily environments. A caring, supportive environment is provided by married couples who serve as teaching-parents and live with a group of approximately 8 youths. These teaching parents, who have received extensive training, assist children and adolescents in learning appropriate behaviors. Token economies and a youth self-government system are some of the means of altering youths' behavior. A major objective of TFM is for the youths to develop adequate skills to enable them to be discharged from the residential treatment setting and be returned to their family when possible. Youths who have participated in these programs have made more positive gains than youth in non-teaching-family residential treatment. Unfortunately, these gains did not persist upon long term release from the treatment program.

In the chapter by Carolyn Webster-Stratton, a set of three programs for parents, teachers and children (ages 3-10 years) is described which is aimed at reducing and preventing conduct problems and drug abuse in children, and promoting their social competence. The model rests upon the assumption that risk factors for later delinquent conduct can be buffered by improving the competencies of children, parents and teachers. The parent training program is conducted in a group setting and teaches skills such as non-violent discipline techniques, problem solving, and effective communication. Videotapes are also included in the program to improve parenting skills. The teacher training program includes motivating through positive reinforcers, strengthening relationships with the students, and increasing problem solving and social skills within the classroom setting. The development of social skills, problem solving, and improved peer interactions is emphasized in the child training program. Outcome studies have demonstrated the effectiveness of this program in terms of improved parent-child interactions, reduced child behavior problems, and increased child problem-solving skills and prosocial behavior. The programs are ideally suited for a school-based intervention.

The importance of a youth's social environment including peers, family, school and neighborhood as a means to reduce behavioral problems is addressed by Scott W. Henggeler in the chapter on Multisystemic Therapy (MST). MST is a family-based treatment, with the underlying assumption that the youth's caregiver is the most likely to influence long term outcomes. Interventions such as behavior therapy, cognitive behavior therapy and family therapy are provided in home, school and community settings. Therapy is usually conducted by teams of therapists who carry case loads of 4 to 6 families for approximately 4 months. In order to disseminate the program more widely, MST has been privatized and has a dedicated faculty and staff of 50 that have facilitated the development of MST programs both nationally and internationally. The programs focus on youth who are at risk of an out-of-home placement because of significant behavioral problems. MST has been shown to reduce days in out-of-home placements and improve emotional and behavioral functioning of youth with serious clinical problems. Juvenile offenders and substance-abusing youths who typically are not compliant with treatment have high rates of treatment completion with the MST program.

In the chapter by John E. Lochman, John F. Curry, Heather Dane, and Mesha Ellis, the Anger Coping Program, an 18-session group cognitive-behavioral intervention, is described. The aim of the program is to improve social-cognitive skills of aggressive children. Although the program was originally designed for young aggressive boys in a school setting, it can be applied with any gender, age and clinical setting. The major features of the program are to help children recognize physiologic signs of anger, to improve perspective-taking, to increase problem-solving skills and to expand the repertoire of appropriate behaviors. A novel aspect of the program is a group project in which the children develop their own videotape to demonstrate the use of problem-solving techniques learned in the program. Children who have participated in the program have shown reduction in aggressive disruptive behavior, improved self-esteem, greater problem-solving skills and lower substance use after treatment and in long term follow-up.

The Aggression Replacement Training (ART) described by Linda A. Reddy and Arnold P. Goldstein is an intervention program designed to prevent aggression in adolescents. It is based on the premise that aggressive behavior is promoted and inhibited by a number of environmental factors (e.g., parents) and internal factors (e.g., social skills). The program consists of three major components aimed at addressing these factors. Skill Streaming uses behavioral techniques such as modeling, role playing, and reinforcement to increase an adolescent's prosocial skills and behaviors. The Anger Control Training component teaches adolescents what not to do in anger-provoking situations, e.g., hit a peer. The third component, Moral Education Training, is designed to increase the level of a child's moral reasoning through group problem solving. Numerous outcome studies have demonstrated the effectiveness of ART in reducing and preventing aggression in adolescents from ethnically diverse backgrounds in a variety of settings, such as juvenile detention facilities.

In the chapter by Kevin J. Moore, Peter G. Sprengelmeyer, and Patricia Chamberlain, a community-based treatment, Multidimensional Treatment Foster Care (MTFC), for adjudicated youth is presented. This intervention program is designed for youth who cannot live in the family home. Prior to placement of the youth in the foster home, foster parents are trained in social learning principles so as to enable these youth to develop skills in family living, social, academic and vocational areas. The aim of the program is to increase the youths' appropriate behaviors so that they are able to return to their parents or to another less restrictive environment. Compared to youths in other care settings, adolescents within the MTFC program have been shown to have a lower re-arrest rate and to be able to return home more often to parents or biological relatives.

Collectively, these eight programs address a wide array of serious emotional and behavioral problems in children and adolescents. The importance of individual, family, school and social factors is emphasized in these programs. These innovative programs can be applied in a broad range of settings such as school, residential treatment centers and juvenile detention facilities. All of the programs have demonstrated effectiveness in treating youths' behavior problems and in promoting prosocial behavior. As illustrated by the authors, selection of a mental health program is based upon the individual needs of the child and family as well as available resources within the community.

Karen Dineen-Wagner, MD

Introduction

Steven I. Pfeiffer, PhD

Many current systems of mental health care fall short of meeting the needs of America's children. All too often, mental health programs lack evidence to support their effectiveness, fail to address the multidimensional nature of serious clinical problems, exclude the natural ecologies of the home, school and neighborhood, don't integrate systems of care, and are extraordinarily expensive. We conceived this project, *Innovative Mental Health Interventions for Children: Programs That Work*, while working on an invited paper on school-based mental health programs in the United States that proposed a tripartite model of mental health interventions (Pfeiffer & Reddy, 1998). One dimension of our tripartite model, *Spectrum of Mental Health Interventions*, includes three levels of preventive interventions (universal, selective and indicated), as well as treatment, maintenance and health promotion/wellness interventions.

With the *Spectrum of Mental Health Interventions* dimension in mind, we selected eight programs for this collection that illustrated a range of innovative prevention, treatment, maintenance and health promotion interventions. Collectively, these model programs offer promising blueprints for reducing a variety of problems in youth, such as aggression, delinquent behavior and substance abuse, sustaining treatment gains and preventing relapse, and promoting resilience, competency and prosocial behavior.

Steven I. Pfeiffer, PhD, is Executive Director of the Talent Identification Program, and Adjunct Professor of Psychology and Education at Duke University.

[Haworth co-indexing entry note]: "Introduction." Pfeiffer, Steven I. Co-published simultaneously in *Residential Treatment for Children & Youth* (The Haworth Press, Inc.) Vol. 18, No. 3, 2001, pp. 1-2; and: *Innovative Mental Health Interventions for Children: Programs That Work* (ed: Steven I. Pfeiffer, and Linda A. Reddy) The Haworth Press, Inc., 2001, pp. 1-2. Single or multiple copies of this article are available for a fee from The Haworth Document Delivery Service [1-800-342-9678, 9:00 a.m. - 5:00 p.m. (EST). E-mail address: getinfo@haworthpressinc.com].

Our selection of programs for inclusion was guided by eight principles. We identified programs that:

- Recognize that there are multiple developmental pathways culminating in a child's increased vulnerability to serious psychological problems;
- Design interventions that target multiple domains and multiple socialization support systems;
- Enhance protective factors such as self-control, affective awareness, social problem-solving, perspective-taking, and positive parenting to strengthen children's social competence;
- Demonstrate clinical effectiveness;
- Are guided by developmental theory;
- Are adaptable to a variety of settings and appropriate for prevention as well as for treatment;
- Provide individualized treatment in accordance with the unique needs of each child;
- Are user-friendly, cost-effective, easy to replicate and emphasize accountability.

Our hope is that *Innovative Mental Health Interventions for Children: Programs That Work* offers the reader a variety of alternative, evidence-based mental health programs that challenge traditional thinking about systems of mental health care for children. We do not endorse any one of the eight programs as *best;* nor do we suggest that our choice of programs is exhaustive. In fact, there are a growing number of innovative programs that meet our above eight principles. If this series sparks debate, challenges some long-held beliefs and affords providers a closer look at what we consider a select group of state-of-the-art mental health programs serving children, then we have accomplished our goal.

REFERENCE

Pfeiffer, S. I., & Reddy, L. A. (1998). School-based mental health programs in the United States: Present status and a blueprint for the future. *School Psychology Review, 27,* 84-96.

I Can Problem Solve (ICPS):
An Interpersonal Cognitive
Problem Solving Program for Children

Myrna B. Shure, PhD

SUMMARY. This article describes an interpersonal problem solving approach to the reduction and prevention of early high-risk behaviors such as aggression, inability to wait and cope with frustration, social withdrawal, and poor peer relations that predict later, more serious problems such as violence, substance abuse, depression, and school dropout. Our research is described that shows that as children as young as age four become more sensitive to their own and others' feelings, more aware of the consequences of their acts, and better able to think of alternative solutions to problems, the early high-risk behaviors can be reduced and prevented. As children move into the elementary grades, decreased emotional distraction also helps them concentrate more efficiently on academic lessons in school. This article describes how a specific intervention for teachers and other school personnel can teach children interpersonal problem solving skills, how the program can fit into the school day, flexibility in delivery of treatment, and other issues of implementation into the school day. Reference is also made to a companion program for parents, an important supplement in light of the national initiative for further parent involvement in the schools. *[Article copies available for a fee from The Haworth Document Delivery Service: 1-800-342-9678. E-mail address: <getinfo@haworthpressinc.com> Website: <http://www.HaworthPress.com> © 2001 by The Haworth Press, Inc. All rights reserved.]*

KEYWORDS. Interpersonal problem solving, high risk aggression, social skill deficits

Myrna B. Shure, PhD, is affiliated with MCP Hahnemann University.

[Haworth co-indexing entry note]: "I Can Problem Solve (ICPS): An Interpersonal Cognitive Problem Solving Program for Children." Shure, Myrna B. Co-published simultaneously in *Residential Treatment for Children & Youth* (The Haworth Press, Inc.) Vol. 18, No. 3, 2001, pp. 3-14; and: *Innovative Mental Health Interventions for Children: Programs That Work* (ed: Steven I. Pfeiffer, and Linda A. Reddy) The Haworth Press, Inc., 2001, pp. 3-14. Single or multiple copies of this article are available for a fee from The Haworth Document Delivery Service [1-800-342-9678, 9:00 a.m. - 5:00 p.m. (EST). E-mail address: getinfo@haworthpressinc.com].

3

MISSION AND OBJECTIVES

The ICPS approach accomplishes three objectives:

1. To teach children *how* to think, not what to think, in ways that will help them resolve typical interpersonal problems with peers and adults.
2. To reduce and prevent early high-risk behaviors such as aggression, inability to wait and cope with frustration, and social withdrawal that predict later, more serious problems such as violence, teen pregnancy, substance abuse, and depression.
3. To help teachers, parents, and other caregivers apply a problem solving style of communication so children can associate how they think with what they do, and how they behave.

HISTORY OF ICPS

In 1968, when my research colleague George Spivack and I began our work together, we were operating out of a mental health center, our mission being to conduct research that would simultaneously serve the needs of our immediate community. Spivack had already developed a cognitive model regarding mental health functioning in adolescents. With the 1960s being the era of "The Great Society" and my own training and background in preschool education, we began to apply Spivack's model with preschool children in community federally-funded day-care centers. We advocated the benefits of initiating mental health services as early as possible in a child's life.

In the 1960s, educational interventions for young children focused on teaching numbers and shapes, and solving impersonal problems such as anagrams (e.g., Davis, 1966). Our approach was different. It focused on problem solving skills that indicated how a person views and handles personal needs or interpersonal situations. Rather than having to solve an abstract puzzle, a person might have to solve the problem of getting what he wants from another person, or of dealing with interpersonal difficulty. The research and intervention was based on our hypothesis that an individual who is overwhelmed by his environment possesses a narrower repertoire of problem solving skills and is preoccupied with the end goal rather than the means to obtain it. If a person is not adept at thinking through ways to solve problems, or if unforeseen obstacles interfere, he or she may make impulsive mistakes, become frustrated and aggressive, or evade the problem entirely by withdrawing. In any case, the individual's initial needs remain unsatisfied, and if such failures occur repeatedly, varying degrees of maladaptive behaviors may ensue.

Having already found that regardless of IQ, one interpersonal cognitive problem solving (ICPS) skill identified by Spivack and Levine (1963) that distinguished impulsive residential treatment home adolescents from those in regular public schools was *means-ends* thinking, or sequential planning. This skill involves an ability to carefully plan means toward a stated interpersonal goal (e.g., making friends), including potential obstacles that could interfere, and an appreciation that problem solving takes time. Shure and Spivack (1972) found that means-ends thinking also distinguished adjustment groups in fifth-graders, and then continued to identify ICPS skills in still younger children. Again regardless of IQ, four- to six-year-olds who displayed impulsive or withdrawn behaviors, and those who were less concerned about other people's feelings were less able than their more socially competent peers to think of *alternative solutions* to problems (such as wanting to play with a toy another child had), and *consequences* to acts (such as hitting the child or grabbing the toy).

To test Spivack's hypothesis that ICPS skills can provide a significant mediator to behavior, Shure developed interventions that would focus on enhancing children's ICPS skills rather than directly on the behaviors themselves. The purpose was to examine whether youngsters who most improved in the trained ICPS skills would also improve most in the behaviors found to be associated with those skills prior to training.

THE INTERVENTIONS

Interventions, originally called Interpersonal Cognitive Problem Solving (ICPS), now called I Can Problem Solve (ICPS), have been designed for ages four through twelve based upon our research identifying the thinking skills with important behaviors relevant to optimal mental health. The underlying approach for all ages is to teach children *how* to think, not what to think, the aim being to help children develop a problem solving thinking "style" that would guide them in coping with everyday problems.

Preschool and kindergarten/primary grades. Originally published in Spivack and Shure (1974), and revised in Shure (1992a), ICPS for younger children consists of sequenced games and dialogues around three levels of language and thinking skills, repeated but upgraded in sophistication in the kindergarten through grade two (Shure, 1992b).

The first level consists of games and dialogues to teach a problem solving vocabulary that can help children later settle disputes. For example, the words *same* and *different* help children later think, "Hitting and kicking are kind of the *same* because they are both ways to hurt people," and then, "I can think of something *different* to do." First, children perform body movements such as tapping their heads and stamping their feet, then identifying whether they are doing the *same* thing or something *different.* In kindergarten, the words *before* and *after* are introduced with questions such as, "Do I brush my teeth *before* or *after* I get out of bed in the morning?" Having associated those words with fun, children can relate to thinking about whether he hit another child *before* or *after* he hit him (or took his toy). While many of the children may understand these concepts, their constant repetition in the early lesson-games helps to establish their use within the framework of interpersonal relations.

The second level of thinking concepts involves words that describe how people feel. In the preschool, those words include *happy, sad, scared,* and *angry,* and words as *frustrated, disappointed, worried, relieved* are added in the kindergarten/primary manual and introduced as children are ready for them. With an understanding of words that designate feelings, it is possible to teach that *different* people feel *different* ways, that feelings change, and that there are ways to find things out–by listening, by watching, and by asking when in doubt. That everybody does not choose the *same* thing is an important concept as young children frequently assume that others like what they like, leading to possible faulty conclusions in interpersonal relations.

The third level consists of the final problem solving skills to be learned–solutions to a problem and consequences to an act. Children may be shown a picture of, for example, a child waiting to come down on a slide, and the child at the bottom won't get off. The group is asked to think of lots of *different* ways the girl at the top can get the boy at the bottom to get off. No value judgment is placed on any particular solution. Having also played games with the words *is/is not,* and *might/maybe,* the next step is for the children to evaluate whether a solution *is* or is *not* a good idea in light of what *"might* happen next."

In addition to the formal didactic lesson-plans, teachers are taught to use the problem solving approach during the day when actual problems arise, a technique we came to call "ICPS dialoguing." Instead of sending children to time-out for not sharing a toy, for example, or suggesting they "play together," children are engaged in the process of thinking about what they do. Questions are asked such as, "How do you think Johnny feels when you grab toys?" "What happened next when you did that?" "How did *you* feel when he did that?" "Can you think of something *different* to do so you both won't feel that way and that won't happen?" Below is an example of a teacher applying "ICPS dialoguing" with two four-year-old boys fighting over a toy.

Teacher: Michael, what's the problem?
(eliciting child's view of the problem)

Michael: I had it first.

Teacher: Richard, what do you think the problem is?

Richard: I had it first.

Teacher: Michael, how do you feel when Richard hits you like that?
(teacher continues the dialogue knowing that she'll never know who had the toy first)

Michael: Mad.

Teacher: And Richard, how do you feel when Michael hits you?

Richard: Mad.

Teacher: What happens when you two hit each other like that?

Richard: We fight.

Teacher: Can you two think of a *different* way to solve this problem so you both won't be mad, and you won't fight?

Michael: We can build an airport (with blocks), I'll be the pilot, and he can be the guy in the back (of the plane).

Instead of ending up in dissatisfaction or frustration, the children were satisfied with their own solution and no more needed to be said.

Although the above dialogue may appear to be somewhat cumbersome and time-consuming, we have observed that children respond to this kind of talk and feel proud because "That was *my* idea." However, after the children become familiar with the approach, the whole dialogue does not have to be used, and can be shortened to, "Can you two think of a *different* way to solve this problem?" or even, "Let's ICPS this."

Intermediate elementary grades. Throughout 15 weeks, the concept "There's more than one way" is stressed to develop a problem solving style of thought. There's more than one way: (a) to *explain* another's *behavior* (e.g., "Maybe he didn't wave because he's mad at me," or, "Maybe he didn't see me."), (b) to *explain* another's *motivation* (e.g., "Maybe that boy [sitting by himself and watching others play] wants to be alone," or, "Maybe others won't let him play."), (c) to *solve a problem* (with different solutions and the more developmentally sophisticated skills of means-ends thinking), and (d) that people might react should a solution or plan be carried out (potential consequences). As in the interventions for younger children, teachers are also trained to apply "ICPS dialoguing" during the day (Shure, 1992c).

KEY TREATMENT INGREDIENTS

How programs fit into school day. In preschool and kindergarten, teachers can implement the formal lesson-games during story time or any time the children are together in a group. It is best to conduct at least one 20-minute lesson daily (for four months) so the concepts become a part of the child's style of thinking. If possible, lessons should be conducted in small groups, allowing for maximum participation from each child. In the grades, teachers have found it possible to substitute ICPS for language arts for the four month period it takes to complete ICPS for a particular grade. They found that children do not lose anything because ICPS *is* language arts, and in fact, standardized achievement test scores go up among ICPS students (Shure, 1993).

Flexibility in delivery of treatment. Because our focus is on *how* children think, not what they think, the *content* of ICPS is a stimulus for the problem solving *process* created for the interventions. Once teachers become comfortable with the program manuals, they are free, even encouraged, to create their own lesson-games content, as long as the *concepts* and their sequence is maintained. Teachers who can create their own ways of conveying the concepts find a feeling of ownership that motivates them to continue ICPS for years to come.

PROGRAM OPERATIONS

Introduction to schools. I have found it most efficient to present a one and one-half hour workshop at a faculty meeting when teachers are already gathered, and then suggesting that only those teachers who are interested participate, at least initially. That way there is no resistance, word will likely spread, and in time, other teachers will want to participate. My belief is that mandating ICPS for a whole school at once not only can create resistance by some teachers, but it is more feasible to build up slowly. One school successfully used a pyramid approach. The school counselor trained the kindergarten through grade one teachers, who in turn trained second through fifth-grade teachers in successive years.

Staffing. It is critical that the classroom teacher be the primary trainer of the children. First, ICPS is a universal intervention, training the whole class, not just high-risk children, because it is a program that can prevent as well as reduce high-risk behaviors (see Research section, below). An outsider who comes into the classroom, implements the formal lessons, and then leaves, creates a situation wherein the teacher does not know how to incorporate the real life "ICPS dialoguing" techniques described earlier. Research has suggested that the formal lessons in the absence of the dialoguing does not help children associate their new problem-solving skills with real life and therefore, does not have the same impact on behavior as it does when both the lesson-games and the dialoguing are used (Weissberg & Gesten, 1982). In addition to the teachers, it is essential that classroom aides also learn the ICPS dialoguing techniques so as not to "undo" what the teacher does. It is important that if the teacher *asks* children for their thoughts and feelings about a situation that the aide does not then *tell* the children what, and what not, to do. It is also very helpful if on-site personnel such as school psychologists or the counselor reinforce the approach with high-risk children whom they see individually. *Training of teachers/on-site personnel.* The ICPS manuals have been designed to be as user-friendly as possible, so that individual teachers can use them without difficulty in their classroom. If desired, training by national ICPS trainers is available, and can occur over a half day, a full day or over a two day period. Ideally, a six-month follow-up is beneficial, though occasional contact by phone, fax or email is often sufficient.

Training/program costs. Training costs $1000 per day, plus travel expenses, although the fee is negotiable depending on individual needs. Each ICPS manual costs $39.95. It is recommended that a leader be familiar with ICPS and adept at working with teachers.

REPLICATION/TRANSPORTABILITY OF PROGRAM

Following our own initial research with African-American youngsters ages 4 through 12 (see Research section below), ICPS has been successfully implemented as research and service programs to thousands of children from various ethnic and income groups nationwide. Examples include Head Starts statewide in Delaware, including Caucasian, African-American, Hispanic, Asian, and American Indian children. An ICPS school in Naperville, Illinois, serves lower- and middle-income Caucasian, African-American, and Oriental kindergarten through fifth-graders. ICPS has been implemented in Head Starts and elementary schools in Alabama, Florida, Tennessee, and Chicago, Illinois. In 1992, the National Mental Health Association of Georgia selected ICPS as their model program, offering ICPS training to its representatives from key local centers and school districts across the state. Because ICPS is a process more than a content, the program is culture-free, and can fit the needs of the population receiving it. It has been reported that the early ICPS vocabulary words helped Hispanic kindergartners learn the English language (Aberson, 1987). Documentation of service evaluations demonstrate significant behavioral gains in ICPS-trained children (Aberson, 1987; Callahan, 1992; Weddle and Williams, 1993).

EVALUATION APPROACH

Our original hypothesis-testing research consisted of age-appropriate testing of each child individually for ability to think of alternative solutions to problems and consequences to acts, and for children ages 8+, for means-ends, sequential planning skills. Each child was also observed by teachers, peers, and/or independent observers for pre-, post-, and followup behaviors as exhibited in the classroom. Most service-evaluations include pre -and post- teacher ratings of behavior only.

SUMMARY OF RESEARCH FINDINGS

Preschool/Kindergarten. Children were studied over a two year period (Shure and Spivack, 1982). In the nursery year, 113 African-American inner-city children (47 boys, 66 girls) were trained, while 106 (50 boys, 56 girls) served as controls. In kindergarten, 69 trained youngsters were still available, 39 who would receive training both years (15 boys, 24 girls), and 30 (123 boys, 18 girls) who would receive no further training (to test for holding power). Of the 62 still-available controls, 35 (15 boys, 20 girls) were first trained in kindergarten, and 27 (12 boys, 15 girls) would constitute the controls. All four groups were initially comparable in age, sex distribution, Binet-IQ (range 70 -147+), and teacher-rated behavioral characteristics.

- Prior to preschool (in the Fall), 36% of the children to be trained were rated as behaviorally *adjusted* (not impulsive or inhibited), and 47% of the controls. Following the intervention (in the Spring), 71% of the trained youngsters were rated adjusted, compared to only 54% of the controls.
- Of the 44 trained children rated as *impulsive* prior to the intervention and 39 controls, 50% of the trained became adjusted compared to only 31% of the controls.
- Of the 28 initially *inhibited* trained children and 17 controls, 75% became adjusted, only 35% controls.
- Of the 35 initially *adjusted* children first trained in kindergarten and the 27 controls, 83% of those trained were adjusted following training, only 30% controls. Of 20 trained youngsters initially showing either *impulsive or inhibited* behaviors and 16 controls, 70% were rated as adjusted in the Spring, and only 6% controls.

- At six-month follow-up, 71% of the 80 still-remaining children adjusted at the end of preschool remained adjusted, compared to 42% of the 65 comparable controls, and one full year later, with 30 trained and 27 nontrained, 77% of the trained retained their adjusted behavior vs. only 30% of the controls.

The behavior gains together with the ICPS score gains being in the same children suggests that the behavior gains were associated with gains in the trained ICPS skills, especially alternative solution skills, and the gains were not explained by initial IQ nor IQ change. The percentage of adjusted controls tending to decrease by the end of the two year period suggests the possibility that impact of ICPS intervention can reverse that trend.

Grades 5 and 6. While it took only one three month exposure to decrease *negative* behaviors in preschool and kindergarten, it took a repeated exposure (in both grades 5 and 6) to decrease these behaviors in older children, also low-income, African-American youngsters. However, nontrained controls showed *more negative* behaviors from grade 5 to grade 6, again suggesting a preventive impact of ICPS intervention (Shure and Healey, 1993).

Positive, prosocial behaviors (caring, sharing, cooperating) improved after only one four month exposure (in grade 5). Standardized achievement test scores and reading grade book levels also improved. Although there was no direct teaching of these academic skills, perhaps behavioral gains allowed the children to focus more on the task-oriented demands of the classroom.

Five year longitudinal study. Of 252 low-income, African-American youngsters available from kindergarten through grade 4, children trained in kindergarten and grade 1 were showing the fewest impulsive and withdrawn behaviors in grade 4, three years after completion of the training, while those trained in kindergarten-only were also showing significantly fewer high-risk behaviors than never-trained controls (Shure, 1993).

Parent training. A companion ICPS program for families (Shure, 1996ab) has also shown that low-income African-American mothers can also be effective training agents, and those who best learned to apply ICPS dialoguing at home had children who showed the most gains in behavior both immediately and as measured three years following the intervention.

CONCLUSIONS

As discussed earlier, impulsivity consists of aggression, and inability to delay gratification and to cope with frustration–significant predictors of later, more serious problems such as violence (a form of hurting others) and substance abuse (a form of hurting oneself). Inhibition consists of inability to stand up for one's rights, and fear and timidity of others–significant predictors of later depression and other forms of mental health dysfunction. ICPS intervention can provide children with skills to think about solving problems important to them when they are very young, and reduce and prevent early high-risk behaviors in ways that will increase their chance of success and social competence in junior high, high school, and beyond.

REFERENCES

Aberson, B. (1996). *An intervention for improving executive functioning and social/ emotional adjustment of ADHD children. Three single case study studies.* Unpublished doctoral dissertation. Miami, FL: Miami Institute of Psychology.

Callahan, C. (1992). *1991-1992 evaluation report for the Mental Health Schools project.* Technical Report. Chicago, IL: Mental Health Association in Illinois.

Davis, G. (1966). Current status of research and theory in human problem solving. *Psychological Bulletin, 66,* 36-54.

Shure, M. B. (1992a). I Can Problem Solve (ICPS): An Interpersonal Cognitive Problem Solving program [preschool]. Champaign, IL: Research Press.

Shure, M. B. (1992b). I Can Problem Solve (ICPS): An Interpersonal Cognitive Problem Solving program [kindergarten/primary grades]. Champaign, IL: Research Press.

Shure, M. B. (1992c). I Can Problem Solve (ICPS): An Interpersonal Cognitive Problem Solving program [intermediate elementary grades]. Champaign, IL: Research Press.

Shure, M. B. (1996a). Raising a Thinking Child. New York: Pocket Books.

Shure, M. B. (2000). Raising a Thinking Child Workbook. Champaign, IL: Research Press.

Shure, M. B., & Healey, K. N. (August, 1993). Interpersonal problem solving and prevention in urban fifth- and sixth-graders. Paper presented at the American Psychological Association, Toronto.

Shure, M. B., & Spivack, G. (1972). Means-ends thinking, adjustment and social class among elementary school-aged children. *Journal of Consulting and Clinical Psychology, 38,* 348-353.

Shure, M. B., & Spivack, G. (1982). Interpersonal problem solving in young children: A cognitive approach to prevention. *American Journal of Community Psychology, 10,* 341-356.

Shure, M. B. (1993). *Interpersonal problem solving and prevention.* A comprehensive report of research and training. #MH-40801. Washington, DC: National Institute of Mental Health.

Spivack, G., & Levine, M. (1963). Self-regulation in acting-out and normal adolescents. Report #M-4531. Washington, DC: National Institute of Health.

Spivack, G., & Shure, M. B. (1974). *Social Adjustment of Young Children.* San Francisco: Jossey-Bass.

Weddle, K. D., & Williams, F. (1993). *Implementing and assessing the effectiveness of the Interpersonal Cognitive Problem-Solving (ICPS) curriculum in four experimental and four control classrooms.* Technical Report. Memphis, TN: Memphis State University.

Weissberg, R. P., & Gesten, E. L. (1982). Considerations for developing effective school-based social problem-solving (SPS) training programs. *School Psychology Review, 11,* 56-63.

The Strengthening Families Program for Young Adolescents: Overview and Outcomes

Virginia Molgaard, PhD
Richard Spoth, PhD

SUMMARY. The Strengthening Families Program: For Parents and Youth 10-14 (SFP 10-14) is a video-based program designed to reduce substance abuse and other problem behavior in youth. Objectives include: (1) building skills in youth to reduce risk and build protective factors, (2) improving parenting practices known to reduce risk in youth, and (3) building stronger family units to support and guide youth. The SFP 10-14 is a universal program designed for ethnically-diverse general populations at all economic and educational levels. The 10 to 14-year-old youth, late elementary and middle school age, attend the program and practice skills together with their parents. *[Article copies available for a fee from The Haworth Document Delivery Service: 1-800-342-9678. E-mail address: <getinfo@haworthpressinc.com> Website: <http://www. HaworthPress.com> © 2001 by The Haworth Press, Inc. All rights reserved.]*

KEYWORDS. Substance abuse, family intervention, video program

Research has shown that transitional periods often increase children's susceptibility to development of problem behaviors. When

Virginia Molgaard, PhD, and Richard Spoth, PhD, are affiliated with the Institute for Social and Behavioral Research, Iowa State University.

[Haworth co-indexing entry note]: "The Strengthening Families Program for Young Adolescents: Overview and Outcomes." Molgaard, Virginia, and Richard Spoth. Co-published simultaneously in *Residential Treatment for Children & Youth* (The Haworth Press, Inc.) Vol. 18, No. 3, 2001, pp. 15-29; and: *Innovative Mental Health Interventions for Children: Programs That Work* (ed: Steven I. Pfeiffer, and Linda A. Reddy) The Haworth Press, Inc., 2001, pp. 15-29. Single or multiple copies of this article are available for a fee from The Haworth Document Delivery Service [1-800-342-9678, 9:00 a.m. - 5:00 p.m. (EST). E-mail address: getinfo@haworthpressinc.com].

youth advance from elementary school to middle school or junior high, they often face social challenges, such as learning to get along with a wider group of peers (Caplan & Weissberg, 1989). It is at this stage, early adolescence, that children are often exposed to substance use for the first time (National Institute on Drug Abuse, 1997). The report of the Carnegie Council on Adolescent Development (1995) characterized this period of development as particularly risky in the context of contemporary society. This is especially true when parenting becomes ineffective. The Strengthening Families Program: For Parents and Youth 10-14 (SFP 10-14) is a scientifically tested program for middle school-aged youth and their parents designed to reduce substance abuse and behavior problems in young people, build skills in parents, and create stronger family units. The seven-session video-based program is appropriate for African American and Hispanic, as well as white, families and has been recognized as an exemplary program by the Office of Juvenile Justice and Delinquency Prevention and the Center for Substance Abuse Prevention, and as a model program by the U.S. Department of Education. The National Institute on Drug Abuse has recognized the program as a scientifically-tested program. In a longitudinal study of the program with 446 families, both youth and parents gained skills. Substance use and aggressive behavior among youth in the intervention condition was significantly lower than it was for youth in the control at follow-up assessment in the 10th grade year, four years post the baseline assessment.

BACKGROUND AND HISTORY OF THE PROGRAM

The SFP 10-14 was developed and evaluated through Project Family, located in the Institute for Social and Behavioral Research at Iowa State University, in cooperation with ISU Extension. Project Family is an "action research" project directed by the second author (see Table 1); it consists of a series of interrelated investigations aimed toward youth and family intervention needs assessments, factors influencing participation in interventions, intervention outcome assessments with both majority and non-majority families, and diffusion of empirically-supported interventions (Spoth, 1999; Spoth & Molgaard, 1999). In 1992, the project received a grant from the National Institute of Mental Health (NIMH) to test the Strengthening Families Program (SFP), developed by Karol Kumpfer and colleagues at the University of Utah

TABLE 1. Program Evaluation

Recommended approach for evaluating in a community setting.
Citations by Spoth and colleagues provided in the references provide detail about prior evaluations of the program. For further recommendations on program evaluation principles and procedures, readers can refer to the following documents and resources:

- Getting to Outcomes: Methods and Tools for Program Evaluation and Accountability (Wandersman et al., 1999 - Contact Abe Wandersman at wandersman@garnet.cla. sc.edu)
- Substance Abuse Among Children and Adolescents: Family Centered Approaches - Practitioner's Guide (Center for Substance Abuse Prevention, 1998 - Contact National Clearinghouse for Alcohol and Drug Information, (800) 729-6686
- Preventing Drug Use Among Children and Adolescents (National Institute on Drug Abuse, 1999 - Contact National Clearinghouse for Alcohol and Drug Information)
- The internet-based "Evaluation Lizard" - Tanglewood Research, Inc., 2000, Greensboro, NC, www.tanglewood.net

Even though the type of research described in the references above provides the most responsible approach to program evaluation, many community groups do not have the funds to carry out these recommended evaluations. Therefore, short instruments for parents and youth are included in the teaching manual in order to obtain information from participants concerning their perceptions about program-induced changes they have made.

(Kumpfer, DeMarsh, & Child, 1989). The study was designed to test the program with a general population of rural families with pre- and young adolescent children. The Project Family investigators, including Karol Kumpfer, agreed that a substantial revision of the SFP was necessary in order to meet the needs of a general population with older children in a Midwestern rural area. The first author worked with Dr. Kumpfer to adapt the SFP, developing a seven-week curriculum identical in format to the original program. That is, the SFP revision also has separate sessions for parents and youth, as well as family sessions in which participants practice skills together in family units.

Based on positive research results from the newly adapted program, called the Iowa Strengthening Families Program (ISFP), the new program was revised so it would be appropriate for ethnically diverse families and renamed as the Strengthening Families Program: For Parents and Youth 10-14. The present version of the curriculum includes seven sessions plus four booster sessions and is currently being tested with African-American and inner-city families.

The theoretical framework for the SFP 10-14 is based on the Biopsychosocial Vulnerability Model (Kumpfer, Trunnel & Whiteside,

1990) and other empirically-based family risk and protective factors (Kumpfer, Molgaard & Spoth, 1996). According to this framework, a key set of psychosocial risk variables are those associated with family attitudes and values interacting with family stressors (e.g., family conflicts, financial stress), and buffered by family coping skills and resources (e.g., effective family management, conflict resolution/problem solving skills, communication skills, social and material support). These family risks, coping skills, and resources are viewed as interacting with community/school and peer-related variables in influencing adolescent adjustment outcomes, including substance abuse and other behavior problems. This theoretical framework assumes a developmental perspective, with the family exerting relatively more influence on pre- and young adolescents than on older adolescents. For more detail on the theoretical basis for the SFP 10-14, see Kumpfer, Molgaard and Spoth, 1996.

PROGRAM FORMAT AND CONTENT

The SFP 10-14 consists of seven sessions plus four booster sessions for parents and youth. The parents and youth attend separate skill-building sessions for the first hour of each session and spend the second hour together in supervised family activities. The program is designed for 8 to 13 families, single parent, two-parent or foster parent. Single parents are invited to ask an extended family member who assists in raising the child (e.g., grandparent, aunt or uncle) to attend with them.

Youth and parent sessions have parallel content during most sessions, with the family session providing reinforcement and skills practice. For example, while the parents are learning about using consequences when youth break rules, youth are learning about the importance of following rules. In the family session that follows, youth and parents practice problem solving as a family for use when rules are broken.

Youth sessions focus on strengthening positive dreams and goals for the future, dealing with stress and strong emotions, appreciating parents and elders, increasing the desire to be responsible, and building skills to deal with peer pressure. Parent sessions include discussions of parents' potential positive influence on pre- and young teens, understanding developmental characteristics of youth this age, providing

nurturing support, dealing effectively with children in everyday interactions, setting appropriate limits, and following through with reason-
able and respectful consequences, as well as sharing beliefs and expectations regarding alcohol and drug use. During the family sessions,
parents and youth practice listening and communicating with respect,
identifying family strengths and family values, using family meetings
to teach responsibility and solve problems and planning fun family
activities. Youth, parent, and family sessions make use of discussions,
skill-building activities, viewing videotapes that model positive behavior, and games designed to build skills and strengthen positive
interactions between family members. (For information on specific
program topics, visit the website at *http://www.exnet.iastate.edu/
Pages/families/sfp.html*)

PROGRAM IMPLEMENTATION

Three group leaders are needed: one to lead the parent session and
two to lead the youth session. The group leader's role changes from
teacher to facilitator during the family sessions and each group leader
takes major responsibility for a subset of 3-4 families, working with
the same families each session. Group leaders must have strong presentation and facilitation skills, experience working with parents and/
or youth, enthusiasm for family skill-building programs and the ability
to be flexible with individuals and activities, within the confines of the
standardized program. Effective group leaders have had a wide-range
of backgrounds and professional interests: teachers, school counselors, family and youth-service workers, mental health staff, Cooperative Extension staff, ministers, and church youth staff and skilled
parents who have previously attended the program.

Appropriate program sites may include schools, social service
agencies, churches, or community centers with at least two rooms, one
large enough for youth and parents together. A television and VCR is
needed for all sessions. Typically the seven sessions are held weekday
nights on consecutive weeks. Optimally the four booster sessions are
held 3-12 months after session seven.

PROGRAM INCENTIVES

Providing meals can be a powerful attendance incentive if there is
grant money to provide them, or if a volunteer group is willing to

prepare food. Busy families may be able to come directly from work and school. If sponsoring groups do not have funds for meals, snacks may be provided during the last 20 minutes of the family session. For some families, having appropriate childcare can make it possible for them to participate and attend regularly. If there are not funds to pay child care workers, facilitators may enlist the support of a church, 4-H, or other club group. Transportation may also be important for some families. Groups may borrow or rent a van or families can be encouraged to share rides. Other incentives that have been used in recruiting and retaining families for the SFP 10-14 are coupons for food treats or groceries or a weekly drawing of food snacks and a family game.

TRAINING

The two-day on-site training includes general information about the background, goals, content, and evaluation of the program. Participants take part in over 100 program activities from parent, youth, and family sessions and receive information on practical considerations for implementing the SFP 10-14, including recommendations for recruitment. After training, consultation and technical assistance by telephone and e-mail for facilitators is available at no cost. Professionals who wish to conduct SFP 10-14 trainings within their organization or city may take part in a train-the-trainer process. For information about this process, contact the first author.

PROGRAM MATERIALS
INCLUDED IN THE TEACHING MANUAL

- A teaching outline as well as a script for the videotapes and detailed instructions for all activities.
- An overview section including information on the background of the program and practical considerations for implementing the SFP 10-14.
- Masters for each worksheet, poster, and handout, including evaluation forms.

Program materials also include the nine videotapes. There are six videos for parent sessions, one for youth sessions five and six, and two for family sessions. Booster sessions require a separate 215-page manual plus two additional booster videos.

RECRUITING AND RETAINING FAMILIES

Program processes for the SFP 10-14 have been designed to recruit and engage both parents and youth in experiential learning and skill building. Effective recruitment for the SFP 10-14 includes: (1) networking with other community agencies, (2) using positive terminology about the program ("Come to help your youth be successful in the teen years."), and (3) personal invitations to families. Program materials and features of the curriculum aid in recruiting and retaining families.

- A promotional videotape and brochure showing families taking part in the program.
- Game-like learning activities and interactive experiences.
- Group support in parent and youth sessions.
- Videotapes showing life-like scenarios of youth and parent interactions.
- Family games and projects.
- A closing circle activity in which parents and youth share one thing they learned at the session.

MAINTENANCE OF SKILLS

Several methods are used to encourage maintenance of skills learned throughout the program. During the final family session, group leaders give a slide show or camcorder presentation, using slides of the youth, parent, and family sessions which were taken over the weeks of the program. Each family is given a framed certificate with a photo of each family for displaying in their home. Also, during the last session, the parents write structured letters to the children related to the content of the program and the youth write similar letters to the parents. These letters are collected by program facilitators and mailed to the families one month after the last session. In addition, several family activities result in posters which participants take with them to display in their home.

DISSEMINATION OF THE PROGRAM

Project Family in cooperation with ISU Extension continues to be involved with scientific tests of the curriculum funded by the National

Institutes of Health. The Extension Service is in charge of the program revisions, duplication, and distribution of the curriculum materials. Extension is also responsible for trainings held in Iowa, while independent contractors provide on-site training outside of Iowa. To date materials have been ordered by organizations in 40 states and on-site trainings have been held in 15 states. Within Iowa over 500 facilitators have been trained and the program has been implemented in over 300 communities. Groups active in disseminating the SFP 10-14 have included cooperative extension, public schools, mental health and social service agencies, churches, substance abuse prevention agencies, and groups working with adjudicated youth through the court system.

PROGRAM COSTS

Program costs include a 415-page teaching manual for each facilitator at $175 each plus one set of nine videotapes at $250 (plus shipping). The two-day training costs $2,500 plus travel, lodging and per diem for two trainers. In addition to teaching manuals, videos, and training costs, implementation costs may include stipends for facilitators, childcare, transportation, and optional meals or snacks. Masters for all handouts, worksheets and teaching games are included in the manual. Thus, there are copying expenses associated with reproducing these items. Program supplies for each family cost approximately $15 per family plus shipping. For information on ordering materials, visit the website at: *http://www.exnet.iastate.edu/Pages/families/sfp.html*

The total costs for the expenses listed above for a group with ten families is estimated at $3000 plus training costs. This figure does not include transportation, room or equipment rental, or food. The costs vary by location, depending on what is appropriate locally as a stipend for facilitators and childcare workers, costs of family supplies, printing, and whether meals or snacks are provided.

SECURING STAKEHOLDERS WITHIN THE COMMUNITY

Securing interest and commitment from sponsoring agencies and groups is the first step in successfully implementing the SFP 10-14. A successful model for involving stakeholders is similar to the recommended method for recruiting families and is outlined below. A group of staff from a social service agency, school, church, family-focused community group or Cooperative Extension, as well as parents from the targeted group, are invited to a one- to two-hour informational meeting. During this meeting participants are shown a five-minute promotional videotape depicting families as they participate in the SFP 10-14. Overheads or posters are shown that highlight features of the program, program topics, and positive outcomes for parents and youth from studies. Next, participants take part in one to three brief program activities to give them a flavor of program content and style. Finally, participants are given a colorful brochure and other written pieces describing the program. They then indicate potential interest in proceeding with the program.

Once stakeholders are secured, the next step is securing funds, either from existing agency budgets, the use of volunteers, or by writing a grant. Information describing the program and research outcomes included in the teaching manual may be used in writing the grant proposal. Additional information which may be used in writing the grant and securing other stakeholders may be obtained from the website: *http://www.exnet.iastate.edu/Pages/families/sfp.html*

PROGRAM FEATURES LENDING TO EASE OF REPLICATION

One of the exceptional features of the Strengthening Families Program: For Parents and Youth 10-14 is the ease of replication. A teaching manual includes detailed instructions for all activities and has masters for all posters and handouts. The manual and its promotional materials received a national award for outstanding educational materials or programs in 1998 by the Agricultural Communicators in Education Information Campaign.

The graphic design of the manual enables facilitators to easily prepare and use the manual during sessions. Each session begins with a cover page that includes a table of contents for the sessions, a detailed list of materials needed and specific session goals. The session outlines have instructional icons to aid facilitators and gives visual illustrations of learning games and activities to help them to implement the curriculum as it is intended.

The use of videotapes in many of the program sessions adds to the ease of replication of the program. Videotapes for all parent sessions, two of the youth sessions, and two of the family sessions help to standardize program delivery, and motivate and improve parent and youth learning by visually demonstrating skillful parent-child and youth peer interactions. The videotapes include timed count-downs for group discussion and activities so that the facilitator starts the video at the beginning of the session which then runs for the entire hour-long parent session. This ensures that each group receives the same content and that the group stays on time and is ready for the family session in the second hour. In addition to the characteristics of the teaching materials that lend themselves to easy replication, training sessions provide facilitators information necessary to implement the program with fidelity.

RESULTS FROM SCIENTIFIC EVALUATION

Following the content revisions to the original SFP and the subsequent feasibility studies, a large-scale prevention trial, including long-term follow-up evaluations, was conducted in 19 counties in the rural Midwest. In addition to a posttest, follow-up data collections were completed approximately 1 1/2, 2 1/2, and 4 years after pretesting. Selected schools were located in rural communities with populations of less than 8,500; these communities had a relatively high percentage of families participating in the school lunch program.

The experimental design entailed random assignment of 33 schools to one of three conditions: (1) the Iowa Strengthening Families Program (ISFP); (2) Preparing for the Drug Free Years (PDFY) (Catalano & Hawkins, 1996), a 5-session youth and family program; or (3) a minimal-contact control condition. Families in the control condition received a set of four parenting guidelines written by Cooperative Extension Service personnel. (See Spoth, Redmond & Shin, 1998, for further information on evaluation design and methods.) The results described below include those from ISFP families and control families.

MEASURES AND DATA COLLECTION

Outcome evaluations entailed the use of multi-informant, multimethod measurement procedures at pretest, posttest, and follow-up data collection points (e.g., see Spoth & Redmond, 1996; Redmond, Spoth, Shin & Lepper, 1999; Spoth, Redmond, & Shin, 1998). Assessments included in-home videotapes of families in structured family interaction tasks, in-home interviews that included scales from a number of standardized instruments.

A total of 161 families participated in 21 ISFP groups at 11 different schools. Groups ranged from 3 to 15 families; the average group consisted of 8 families, an average of 12 adults and 8 youth. Both single parent and two-parent families participated. Among more than half of the two-parent families, both parents attended at least some of the sessions. Ninety-four percent of attending, pretested families were represented by a family member in five or more sessions.

RESULTS

An analysis of data collected in the longitudinal, controlled study demonstrated positive results for both parents and youth. Comparisons between the intervention and control group showed significantly improved parenting behaviors directly targeted by the intervention (e.g., clarification of substance use rules and consequences, increased level of positive parent-child involvements). These behaviors were, in turn, strongly associated with general child management (e.g., standard setting, monitoring, effective discipline) and parent-child affective quality (e.g., expressions of positive affect) (See Russell, Kahn, Spoth & Altmaier, 1998; Spoth, Redmond & Shin, 1998). A test of the intervention change model at the 1 1/2 year follow-up assessment showed similar results (Redmond, Spoth, Shin, & Lepper, 1999). Analyses of youth substance use and use-related child outcomes (e.g., gateway substance use, conduct problems, school-related problem behaviors, affiliation with antisocial peers, peer resistance) have demonstrated positive outcomes at follow-up assessments, as described below (see Figures 1, 2 and 3).

Because of the young age of children in the study, significant intervention-control differences in problem behavior outcomes were expected to be initially detectable at the 1 1/2-year post baseline follow-up and in subsequent assessments. Consistent with this expectation, multilevel ANCOVAs showed significant intervention-control differences in substance use, conduct problems (e.g., physical aggression, minor theft, property damage), school-related problem behaviors (e.g., truancy, cheating), peer resistance, and affiliation with antisocial peers at 1 1/2 and 2 1/2 years following pretesting (Spoth, Redmond, &

Project Family Research Group, 1997; 1998). Detailed analyses of individual substance use behaviors showed noteworthy differences between intervention and control groups. For example, at the 1 1/2-year follow-up there was a 60 percent relative reduction in the first-time use of alcohol without parental permission in the intervention group (Spoth, Redmond, & Lepper, 1999).

In addition, probability of transitioning from nonuse of tobacco,

Substance Use Initiation by ISFP Youth Compared to Control Youth

FIGURE 1. New User Proportions of Alcohol Use by Experimental Condition

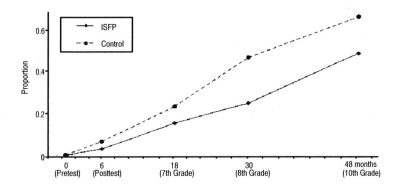

FIGURE 2. New User Proportions of Cigarette Use by Experimental Condition

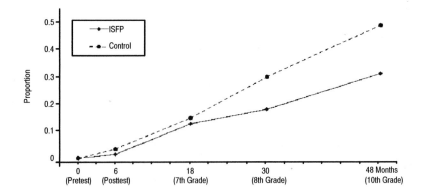

FIGURE 3. New User Proportions of Marijuana Use by Experimental Condition

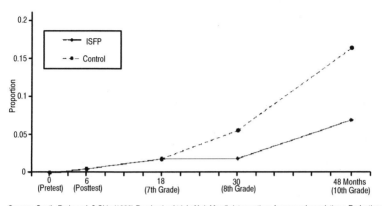

Source: Spoth, Redmond, & Shin (1999) Randomized trial of brief family interventions for general populations: Reductions in adolescent substance abuse four years following baseline. Manuscript under review.

alcohol, or other drugs was examined. Findings suggested that ISFP group children who had not initiated substance use at the 1 1/2 year follow-up assessment were significantly less likely to initiate use by the 2 1/2 year follow-up assessment than were control group children (Spoth, Reyes, Redmond, & Shin, 1999). Finally, recent analyses of substance use initiation and regular use (alcohol, tobacco, and marijuana) and other problem behaviors (hostile and aggressive behaviors) at 4 years post baseline have also shown positive results. Specifically, as compared with youth in the control group, those in the ISFP group showed significantly delayed initiation of alcohol, tobacco and marijuana use (Spoth, Redmond & Shin, 1999a), lower frequency of alcohol and cigarette use (Spoth, Redmond & Shin, 1999a), lower levels of overt and covert aggressive behaviors and hostility in interactions with parents (Spoth, Redmond & Shin, 1999b). (See Figures 1-3 for comparison of intervention and control group substance use initiation rates across data collection points.)

REFERENCES

Botvin, G. J. (1996). *The Life Skills Training.* Princeton, NJ: Princeton Health Press, Inc.

Caplan, M., & Weissberg, R.P. (1989). Promoting social competence in early adolescence: Developmental considerations. In B.H. Schneider, G. Attili, J. Nadel, & R.P.

Weissberg (Eds.), *Social competence in developmental perspective* (pp. 371-385). Boston: Kluwer Academic.

Carnegie Council on Adolescent Development. (1995). *Great transitions: Preparing adolescents for a new century.* New York: Carnegie Council of New York.

Cztzlono, R. F. & Hawkins, J. D. (1996). The social development model: A theory of antisocial behavior (Ed.), *Delinquency and crime: Current theories* (pp. 149-197) Cambridge University Press.

Hawkins, J.D., Catalano, R.F., & Miller, J.Y. (1992). Risk and protective factors for alcohol and other drug problems in adolescence and early adulthood: Implications for substance abuse prevention. *Psychological Bulletin, 112*(1), 64-105.

Kumpfer, K. L., Trunnell, E. P., & Whiteside, A. O. (1990). The biopsychosocial model: Application to the addictions field. In R. C. Engs (Ed.) *Controversy in the Addiction Field.* Dubuque, IA: Kendall/Hunt Publishing Co., 55-66.

Kumpfer, K.L., DeMarsh, J.P., & Child,W. (1989). *Strengthening Families Program: Children's skills training curriculum manual, parenting training manual, children's skill training manual, and family skills training manual* (Prevention Services to Children of Substance-Abusing Parents). Salt Lake City: University of Utah, Social Research Institute, Graduate School of Social Work.

Kumpfer, K.L., Molgaard,V., & Spoth, R. (1996). The Strengthening Families Program for the prevention of delinquency and drug use. In R.D. Peters & R.J. McMahon (Eds.), *Preventing childhood disorders, substance abuse, and delinquency* (pp. 241-267). Thousand Oaks, CA: Sage.

Molgaard, V. K., Kumpfer, K. L., & Fleming, E. (1997 revised). *The Strengthening families program: For parents and Iowa youth 10-14 leader guide.* Ames, IA: Iowa State University Extension.

National Institute on Drug Abuse. (1997). *Preventing drug use among children and adolescents: A researched-based guide* (NIH Publication No. 97-4212). Rockville, MD: Author.

Redmond, C., Spoth, R., Shin, C., & Lepper, H. (in press). Modeling long-term parent outcomes of two universal family-focused preventive interventions: One year follow-up results. *Journal of Consulting and Clinical Psychology, 67*(6), 975-984.

Russell, D. W., Kahn, J., Spoth, R., & Altmaier, E. M. (1998). Analyzing data from experimental studies: A latent variable structural equation modeling approach. *Journal of Counseling Psychology, 45*(1), 18-29.

Spoth, R., Redmond, C. & Project Family Research Group (1997). *Rural youth at risk: Extension-based prevention efficacy.* Unpublished manuscript. Proposal for grant funded by National Institute of Mental Health.

Spoth, R., Redmond, C. & Project Family Research Group (1998). *Rural family and community drug abuse prevention project.* Unpublished manuscript. Proposal for grant funded by National Institute on Drug Abuse.

Spoth, R. (1999). Family-focused preventive intervention research: A pragmatic perspective on issues and future directions. In R. Ashery, E. Robertson, & K. Kumpfer (Eds.), *NIDA Research Monograph on drug abuse prevention through family interventions* (pp. 459-510). Rockville, MD: National Institute on Drug Abuse.

Spoth, R., & Molgaard, V. (1999). Project Family: A partnership integrating research with the practice of promoting family and youth competencies. In T.R. Chibucos & R. Lerner (Eds.), *Serving children and families through community-university partnerships: Success stories.* (pp. 127-137). Boston: Kluwer Academic.

Spoth, R. & Redmond, C. (1996). A theory-based parent competency model incorporating intervention attendance effects. *Family Relations, 45,* 139-147 (special issue on family-related preventive interventions).

Spoth, R., Redmond, C., & Lepper, H. (1999). Alcohol initiation outcomes of universal family-focused preventive interventions: One- and two-year follow-ups of a controlled study. *Journal of Studies on Alcohol* [Invited article for special issue on alcohol and the family], (Suppl. 13), 103-111.

Spoth, R., Redmond, C., & Shin, C. (1998). Direct and indirect latent-variable parenting outcomes of two universal family-focused preventive interventions: Extending a public health-oriented research base. *Journal of Consulting and Clinical Psychology, 66*(2), 385-399.

Spoth, R., Redmond, C., & Shin, C. (1999a). *Randomized trial of brief family interventions for general populations: Reductions in adolescent substance use four years following baseline.* Manuscript under review.

Spoth, R., Redmond, C., & Shin, C. (1999b). *Reducing adolescents' hostile and aggressive behaviors: Randomized trial affects of a brief family intervention four years past baseline.* Manuscript under review.

Spoth, R., Reyes, M.L., Redmond, C., & Shin, C. (1999). Assessing a public health approach to delay onset and progression of adolescent substance use: Latent transition and loglinear analyses of longitudinal family preventive intervention outcomes. *Journal of Consulting and Clinical Psychology, 67*(5), 619-630.

The Incredible Years:
Parents, Teachers,
and Children Training Series

Carolyn Webster-Stratton, PhD

SUMMARY. This article summarizes the Incredible Years Training Series which consists of three empirically validated and integrated programs for parents, teachers and children that are designed to promote social competence and prevent, reduce and treat conduct problems in young children ages 3 to 8 years. This summary explains the risk and protective factors related to the early development of conduct problems and describes how these interventions address those risk factors which are malleable. The training methods, content, and processes are explained. Finally, the highlights of selected studies of each of these programs is presented. *[Article copies available for a fee from The Haworth Document Delivery Service: 1-800-342-9678. E-mail address: <getinfo@ haworthpressinc.com> Website: <http://www.HaworthPress.com> © 2001 by The Haworth Press, Inc. All rights reserved.]*

KEYWORDS. Promoting social competence, at risk children, parent/ teacher training

Carolyn Webster-Stratton is affiliated with the University of Washington.

All of these studies have been supported by several grants including: Child and Adolescent Treatment and Preventive Research Branch of the National Institute of Mental Health, 5R01 MH5-516; a Research Scientist Award, MH00988, from NIMH; Administration for Children and Families, Head Start Partnership Grant, 90-CD-0949; the National Center for Nursing Research Grant R01 NR01075; and a SAMH-SA/CSAP grant, 5UR6 SP07960.

[Haworth co-indexing entry note]: "The Incredible Years: Parents, Teachers, and Children Training Series." Webster-Stratton, Carolyn. Co-published simultaneously in *Residential Treatment for Children & Youth* (The Haworth Press, Inc.) Vol. 18, No. 3, 2001, pp. 31-45; and: *Innovative Mental Health Interventions for Children: Programs That Work* (ed: Steven I. Pfeiffer, and Linda A. Reddy) The Haworth Press, Inc., 2001, pp. 31-45. Single or multiple copies of this article are available for a fee from The Haworth Document Delivery Service [1-800-342-9678, 9:00 a.m. - 5:00 p.m. (EST). E-mail address: getinfo@haworthpressinc.com].

MISSION AND OBJECTIVES OF THE PROGRAM

The Incredible Years: Parents, Teachers, and Children Training Series, developed by Professor Carolyn Webster-Stratton at the University of Washington, is a comprehensive set of programs designed to promote social competence and prevent, reduce, and treat aggression and related conduct problems in young children (ages 3 to 10 years). The three types of interventions that make up this series–parent training, teacher training, and child training–are guided by developmental theory concerning the role of multiple interacting risk and protective factors (child, family, and school) in the development of conduct problems. Over the past 20 years, these programs have been evaluated in six randomized control group studies as treatment programs for children diagnosed with Oppositional Defiant Disorder (ODD) and Conduct Disorder (CD). Adapted versions of these programs have been evaluated in three randomized studies as school-based prevention programs with high-risk, multi-ethnic populations, namely, Head Start and day care teachers, parents, and children. The programs have been replicated by other independent investigators (e.g., Spaccarelli, Cotler, & Penman, 1992; Taylor, Schmidt, Pepler, & Hodgins, 1998) and are empirically validated to accomplish the three objectives.

Objective one, *Promote Child Social Competencies*, consists of strengthening children's social skills and appropriate play skills, promoting problem solving skills and anger management strategies, increasing self-esteem, boosting academic success and reading readiness, reducing defiance, aggressive behavior, and related conduct problems (e.g., noncompliance, peer bullying, rejection), decreasing children's negative attributions, and increasing empathy skills.

Objective two, *Promote Parent Competencies and Strengthen Families*, consists of increasing parenting and communication skills, reducing critical and violent discipline approaches with positive strategies (e.g., ignoring, use of natural consequences, redirection), improving parents' problem-solving skills and anger management, increasing family support networks and school involvement, and helping parents and teachers work collaboratively. Objective three, *Promote Teacher Competencies and Strengthen Home-School Connections*, consists of strengthening teachers' effective classroom management skills, including proactive teaching approaches such as use of effective discipline strategies, collaboration between home and school, and training of social skills, anger management, and problem-solving skills in the classroom. The long-term goal of these early prevention programs is to reduce violence, drug abuse, and delinquency in later years.

Program Rationale

The problem. The incidence of aggression in children is escalating– and at younger ages. Studies indicate that anywhere from 7-20% of preschool and early school age children meet the diagnostic criteria for ODD and CD. These rates may be as high as 35% for low-income welfare families (Webster-Stratton & Hammond, 1998). Research on the treatment and prevention of conduct disorders has been identified as one of the nation's highest priorities (NIMH, 1996). This agenda is vitally important because of the widespread occurrence of delinquency and escalating adolescent violence with its resulting high cost to society. Emergence of "early onset" ODD/CD in preschool children (in the form of high rates of oppositional defiance and aggressive and noncompliant behaviors) is stable over time and appears to be the single most important behavioral risk factor for antisocial behavior in adolescence (Dishion, French, & Patterson, 1995). Such behavior has repeatedly been found to predict the development of drug abuse in adolescence (Dishion & Ray, 1991) as well as other problems such as juvenile delinquency, depression, violent behavior, and school drop-out. Moreover, since conduct disorder becomes increasingly resistant to change over time, intervention that begins in the early school years is clearly a strategic way to prevent substance abuse, delinquency, and mental illness in adolescence. Unfortunately, recent projections suggest that fewer than 10% of the children who need mental health services for ODD/CD actually receive them (Hobbs, 1982). Less than half of those receive "empirically validated" or "evidence based" interventions (Chambless & Hollon, 1998).

Risk factors. There are multiple risk factors (community, school, family, parent, and child) contributing to the development of CD in children and to the subsequent development of violence and drug abuse. Nonetheless, it is evident from the research that there are no clear-cut causal links between single factors and the child's social adjustment. Most of these factors are intertwined, synergistic, and cumulative. Multiple risk factors result in an unfolding cycle of events over time with cumulative effects on a child's vulnerability (Coie et al.,

1993). Consequently, prevention programs need to target multiple risk factors at strategic time points, particularly those that offer potential for change. Enhancing protective factors such as positive parenting and teaching skills, parent involvement with schools as well as other support systems and interventions that strengthen children's social competence and school readiness will help buffer against the development of conduct problems. For a review of risk factors related to the development of conduct problems, please see Webster-Stratton and Hooven, 1998.

Intended Population

These programs may be offered as universal, selected, and indicated prevention interventions within schools, churches, mental health agencies, and health maintenance organizations. Targeted populations include: (1) Parents and teachers who work with average and high-risk children (ages 3 to 10), (2) Parents of children with conduct problems (ages 3 to 10), (3) Preschool, day care and early elementary teachers of students with conduct problems, (4) Parents at risk for abuse or neglect, and (5) Teenagers taking babysitting classes or family life courses.

KEY INGREDIENTS OF PROGRAMS

Highlights of Parent, Teacher, and Child Training Series include: (1) comprehensiveness (includes integrated training for parents, teachers, and children), (2) a proactive, collaborative approach, (3) flexibility in delivery using sequenced modules (26 topics in total), (4) culturally sensitive (available in Spanish and in British dialect, multi-ethnic videotapes and puppets), (5) appropriate for prevention programs for mainstream children, as well as for treatment for children diagnosed with conduct problems, (6) user-friendly–uses a combination of books, videotapes, leader manuals, and home and school activities, (7) developmentally appropriate for young children–includes puppets, games, and activities, (8) provides extensive program support for training therapists, school personnel, and organizations, including the crucial group leader training, (9) provides certification for trainers to assure quality implementation, and (10) evidence-based and replicated by independent researchers.

Program Description–Parent Training Programs

The BASIC parent training series, a 12-week program for parents, involves group discussion of a series of 250 video vignettes. The program teaches parents interactive play and reinforcement skills, nonviolent discipline techniques, including "Time Out" and "ignore," logical and natural consequences, and problem-solving strategies. Brief videotaped vignettes of parents interacting with children in family life situations illustrate childrearing concepts. Group leaders use these scenes to facilitate group discussion and problem solving. Participants discuss the principles of childrearing and practice new skills through role-playing and home practice activities. The program, which can be self-administered or offered for groups of 10 to 14 participants, can be covered in 12 to 14, 2-hour weekly sessions.

The ADVANCE parent training series is a 12-week supplement to the BASIC program that addresses other family risk factors such as depression, marital discord, poor coping skills, and lack of support. Topics include personal self-control, effective communication strategies and problem-solving between adults and children. The program takes 8 to 12, 2-hour sessions to complete.

The SCHOOL AGE parent training series addresses a more culturally diverse population and is intended for use as a prevention-oriented program with children up to age 9 or 10 (grade 4). In conjunction with this, a new program, SUPPORTING YOUR CHILD'S EDUCATION, teaches parents ways to strengthen their children's reading and academic readiness, to set up predictable home learning activities, and to promote strong connections between home and school (see Figure 1).

The parent training program materials include: (1) 10 videotapes for the BASIC program (available in Spanish), (2) 6 videotapes for the ADVANCE program, (3) 2 videotapes for the SUPPORTING YOUR CHILD'S EDUCATION training program, (4) 3 videotapes for the school-age version of BASIC, (5) Self-administered manual for the BASIC program, (6) Comprehensive leader manuals for each program (consisting of over 500 pages of "how to," including leader questions for discussion, home activities, and interpretation of videotapes), (7) Parent weekly "refrigerator notes" (brief points to remember), (8) Parent assignments for home activities, (9) Book for parents entitled, *The Incredible Years: A Trouble-Shooting Guide for Parents of Children*

FIGURE 1. Parenting Pyramid

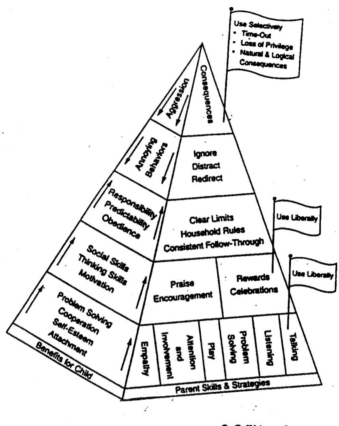

© C. Webster-Stratton

Ages 3-8 (also available on audiotape), and (10) Refrigerator magnets and pyramid poster. All the programs use multiple learning approaches: videotape modeling, group discussion and support, practice activities within sessions, home activities, reading assignments (or audiotapes), self-monitoring checklists and goals, and leader teaching/ support. The programs are highly interactive, collaborative, and self-directed.

Training Methods

The parent programs are designed as group discussions with 12 to 14 parents per group and 1 group leader (2 leaders if resources permit). The group format fosters a sense of community support, reduces isolation, and normalizes parents' experiences and situations. This cost-effective approach also allows for diverse experiences with problem solving in a variety of family situations. Each parent is encouraged to have a partner or close friend participate in the program.

Videotape modeling. Modeling theories of learning suggest that parents can improve parenting skills by watching videotaped examples of parents interacting with their children in ways that promote prosocial behaviors and decrease inappropriate behaviors. This method of training is more accessible, especially to less verbally oriented parents, than other methods such as didactic instruction, written handouts, or a sole reliance on group or individual discussion. It promotes generalization and long-term maintenance of positive behaviors by portraying a variety of models in many situations.

Collaborative process. In this collaborative training model, the leader is not an "expert" who dispenses advice to parents. Meaning "to labor together," collaboration implies a reciprocal relationship that uses the leader's and parents' knowledge, strengths, and perspectives equally. In this nonblaming and nonhierarchical model, the leader promotes collaboration through reflection, summary of points made by parents, reframing, reinforcement, support and acceptance, humor and optimism, encouragement of each member's participation, teaching of important concepts, and role-playing exercises. By using a collaborative process, the program becomes culturally sensitive as each individual's personal goals and values are respected, and "connections" with the past are relevant to current perspectives and attitudes. Approximately 60 percent of a session is group discussion, problem solving, and support; 25 percent is videotape modeling (25 to 30 minutes of videotape); and 15 percent is teaching. More information about collaborative process can be found in the following books: Webster-Stratton and Hancock, 1998; Webster-Stratton and Herbert, 1994.

Resources needed. In order for parent groups to be well attended, group leaders need to have available day care with qualified day care providers, transportation for those who need it, healthy food and a room large enough for a circle of 14 people. Evening meetings are necessary in order to make it possible for two parents to participate. VCRs and blackboards or flip charts are required.

Program Description–Teacher Training Program

This program includes six components: The Importance of Teacher Attention, Encouragement, and Praise; Motivating Children Through Incentives; Preventing Problems–The Proactive Teacher; Decreasing Inappropriate Behavior; Building Positive Relationships with Students; and Social Skills and Problem Solving Training in the Classroom. The teaching concepts are illustrated with brief videotaped vignettes of teachers interacting with children in classrooms which include large classrooms with 28 children and 1 teacher and smaller special education classrooms with multiple teachers. As with the parent programs, group leaders use these videotaped scenes to facilitate discussion, problem solving, and sharing ideas among teachers.

Training methods. The collaborative training methods used with teacher training groups are similar to those used with parent groups. Teachers come together in groups of 15 to 25 to discuss a series of vignettes. It takes 6 full-day workshops to complete all 6 components of the training. This training may be offered 1 day a month or in weekly 2-hour sessions (18-20 weeks).

Dina Dinosaur Social Skills and Problem-Solving Curriculum–Child Training Programs

Intervening at a young age can help children develop effective social skills early and reduce their aggressive behaviors before these behaviors develop into permanent patterns. Although parent training is likely to affect parent-child relationships at home, it is less likely to impact peer relationships. To address peer problems, children must receive training in social skills/problem solving, and trained teachers must reinforce the use of such skills at school (Webster-Stratton & Hammond, 1997).

The Dina Dinosaur Social Skills and Problem-Solving Curriculum is designed to enhance children's school behaviors, to promote social competence and positive peer interactions, to develop appropriate conflict management strategies, and to reduce conduct problems. In addition, the program was organized to dovetail with the parent and teacher training programs. For treatment of children with conduct problems, the program is offered to groups of five to six children in 2-hour sessions held once a week for 18 to 22 weeks. For use as a classroom-wide prevention program, the program can be offered in 15- to 20-minute, large group circle time sessions, supplemented with small group practice activities, several times a week. Part 6 of the teacher training series shows teachers how they can use this curriculum as a prevention program (preschool-second grade).

Training methods. Methods for teaching social skills to young children must be commensurate with the children's learning styles, temperaments, and cognitive and developmental abilities. Training programs for older children often require verbal and cognitive skills that early school age children do not have. This program makes use of the following approaches: videotape modeling; fantasy play; use of near life-sized puppets (Wally & Molly) who get help from children for problems such as being teased or bullied by others, feeling left out, lying and stealing, being afraid and anxious and making new friends; role playing; practice activities, games, and children's books; Wally's detective club home activity manual; and parent and teacher involvement.

DISSEMINATION INGREDIENTS

Program Features Lending to Ease of Replication/ Independent Replication Studies

The videotape format of the training programs increases the consistency, fidelity, and transportability of the program implementation, making it easier and less costly to implement in real-world settings. All the programs include detailed leader manuals, handouts, books, videotapes, information about the group process, and activities which facilitate the replicability of the program.

Training and Qualifications of Group Leaders

Group leaders may come from many disciplines, including nursing, psychology, counseling, social work, education, and psychiatry. We find that the program has a greater chance of being disseminated successfully if the group leaders receive one of our authorized training programs. We also highly recommend certification for the group leaders in order to enhance the quality and integrity of the programs. This certification requires participants to attend training workshops that are offered regularly in Seattle or on-site (if there are a minimum of 25 participants). Group leader certification is required if the program is to be evaluated as part of a research program.

EVALUATION OUTCOMES

First the BASIC program was evaluated as a treatment program in a series of six randomized studies with more than 800 children ages 3 to 7 referred for conduct problems. These studies have shown that the BASIC program results in significantly improved parental attitudes and parent-child interactions, reduced parents' use of violent forms of discipline, and reduced child conduct problems (Webster-Stratton, 1984; Webster-Stratton, 1989; Webster-Stratton, 1990b; Webster-Stratton, Hollinsworth, & Kolpacoff, 1989). The ADVANCE program has been shown to be a highly effective treatment for promoting parents' use of effective problem-solving and communication skills, reducing maternal depression, and increasing children's social and problem-solving skills. Users have been highly satisfied with both programs, and the dropout rates have been low regardless of the family's socioeconomic status. Effects have been sustained up to 4 years after intervention (Webster-Stratton, 1990b).

Next, the BASIC program was evaluated as a universal prevention program in two randomized trials with over 500 Head Start families. Results indicated that the parenting skills of Head Start parents who received training and the social competence of their children significantly improved compared with the control group. These data supported the hypothesis that strengthening parenting competence and increasing parental involvement of high-risk welfare mothers in children's school-related activities will help prevent children's conduct problems and promote social competence (Webster-Stratton, 1998). These findings were independently replicated in a study in Chicago with daycare providers and low-income, African American mothers with toddlers (Gross, Fogg, & Tucker, 1995).

Highlights of Selected Studies of the BASIC Program

Indicated prevention. This study was conducted to ascertain the most effective component of the BASIC program. Parents of 114 conduct-problem children, ages 3 to 8, were randomly assigned to one of four groups: (1) Individually or self-administered videotape modeling therapy (IVM); (2) Videotape-based group therapy (BASIC); (3) Group therapy alone (GD), and (4) Waiting-list control group. Compared with the control group, mothers in all three treatment groups reported significantly fewer child behavior problems, more prosocial behaviors, and less use of spanking following treatment. Fathers in the IVM and BASIC groups, and teachers of children whose parents were in the BASIC and GD groups, also reported significant reductions in behavior problems compared with control subjects. Data collected from home visits indicated that, for all treatment groups, mothers, fathers, and children exhibited significant behavioral changes. Differences found consistently favored BASIC treatment. Cost-effectiveness, however, was the major advantage of the IVM treatment (Webster-Stratton, 1990b; Webster-Stratton, Kolpacoff, & Hollinsworth, 1988). At the 1-year follow-up, 93.1 percent of families were assessed. All significant behavioral changes reported immediately after treatment were maintained. Moreover, parent report data indicated that both parents perceived a further reduction in child behavior problems. Results indicated that the BASIC treatment was superior. With each of the programs, 70 percent of the sample showed clinically significant improvements to within normal ranges (Webster-Stratton et al., 1989).

Indicated prevention. Another study was conducted to determine how to enhance the effectiveness of the self-administered videotape therapy while maintaining its cost-effectiveness. Parents of 43 conduct-problem children were assigned to one of three groups: (1) IVM; (2) IVM plus therapist consultation (IVMC); and (3) Waiting-list control group. In comparison with the control group, both groups of mothers receiving treatment reported significantly fewer child behavior problems, reduced stress levels, and less use of spanking after intervention. Data from home visits indicated that both treatment groups exhibited significant behavioral changes. IVMC children in the videotape plus therapist consultation group were significantly less deviant than the children in the individually administered videotape program, suggesting that combined treatment was superior (Webster-Stratton, 1990a).

Selective prevention. In this study we examined the effectiveness of the BASIC program as a universal, school-based prevention program with a sample of 362 Head Start mothers and their 4-year-old children. Eight Head Start centers were randomly assigned to two groups: (1) An experimental group in which parents, teachers, and family service workers participated in the intervention and in the regular center-based Head Start program; and (2) A control group in which parents, teachers, and family service workers only participated in the regular center-based Head Start program. The results from observations at the post-intervention assessment indicated that mothers in the intervention group used less harsh discipline and were more nurturing, reinforcing, and competent in their parenting when compared with mothers in the control group. In turn, the children of mothers in the intervention group exhibited significantly fewer conduct problems and more positive affect and prosocial behaviors than children in the control group. One year later, most of the improvements were maintained, including increased contacts with new teachers, as compared with mothers in the control group (Webster-Stratton, 1998).

Selective prevention. Recently we examined the effectiveness of the BASIC program combined with our teacher training program with a sample of 272 Head Start mothers and 61 teachers. Results replicated the earlier Head Start study in terms of behavioral improvements for mother-child behaviors. Results of classroom observations indicated that teachers in the intervention group were significantly less critical and more positive in their discipline approaches than teachers in the control group. Teachers from the intervention condition reported making significantly more effort to involve parents in their classrooms. Students in intervention classrooms were observed to exhibit significantly fewer negative behaviors and noncompliance with teachers and less physical aggression with peers than students in control classrooms. Intervention children were more engaged or on-task in the classroom and had higher school readiness scores (e.g., friendly, self-reliant, on task, low disruptive) than control children. Overall classroom atmosphere was significantly more positive for intervention classrooms than control classrooms. Intervention students were observed more socially competent than the control students.

Study of the ADVANCE Program

Indicated prevention. This study examined the effects of adding the ADVANCE intervention component to the BASIC intervention. Parents of 78 families with children with ODD/CD (conduct disorder) received the BASIC parent training and then were randomly assigned to either ADVANCE training for 12 weeks or no further contact. For both treatment groups, child adjustment and parent-child interactions significantly improved and parent distress and child behavior problems decreased. These changes were maintained at follow-up. ADVANCE children showed significant increases in the total number of solutions generated during problem solving, most notably in prosocial solutions as compared to aggressive solutions, in comparison with their counterparts. Observations of parents' marital interactions indicated significant improvements in ADVANCE parents' communication, problem solving, and collaboration when compared with parents who did not receive ADVANCE training. Only one family dropped out of the ADVANCE program, which attests to its perceived usefulness by families.

Study of Child Training–
Dina Dinosaur Curriculum

Indicated prevention. The Dina Dinosaur curriculum for children was evaluated in a randomized trial with conduct-disordered children ages 4 to 7. Families of 97 children with early-onset conduct problems were randomly assigned to one of four groups: (1) Child training only; (2) Parent training only (BASIC & ADVANCE); (3) Combined parent/child training intervention, and (4) Waiting-list control.

Results showed that the combined parent and child training was more effective than parent training alone and that both were superior to the control group. The child training program resulted in significant improvements in observations of peer interactions. Children who had received the Dinosaur curriculum were significantly more positive in their social skills and conflict management strategies than children whose parents got parent training only or than controls. One year later the combined parent and child intervention showed the most sustained effects (Webster-Stratton & Hammond, 1997).

Ongoing Studies of Academic Skills Training
for Parents and Training for Teachers

Currently in progress is a randomized study in which families are assigned to one of six groups involving the various combinations of child, parent, and teacher training. Preliminary results suggest that combining academic skills training for parents with training for teachers improves children's outcomes in terms of strengthening both academic and social skills, promoting more positive peer relationships, and assuring behavior problems are reduced at school and at home.

REFERENCES

Chambless, D. L., & Hollon, S. D. (1998). Defining empirically supported therapies. *Journal of Consulting and Clinical Psychology, 66,* 7-18.

Coie, J. D., Watt, N. F., West, S. G., Hawkins, D., Asarnow, J. R., Markman, H. J., Ramey, S. L., Shure, M. B., & Long, B. (1993). The science of prevention: A conceptual framework and some directions for a national research program. *American Psychologist, 48,* 1013-1022.

Dishion, T. J., French, D. C., & Patterson, G. R. (1995). The development and ecology of antisocial behavior. In D. Cicchetti & D. J. Cohen (Eds.), *Developmental psychopathology, Vol 2: Risk disorder and adaptation* (pp. 421-471). New York: Wiley.

Dishion, T. J., & Ray, J. (1991). *The development and ecology of substance abuse in adolescent boys* (Unpublished): Oregon Social Learning Center.

Gross, D., Fogg, L., & Tucker, S. (1995). The efficacy of parent training for promoting positive parent-toddler relationships. *Research in Nursing and Health, 18,* 489-499.

Hobbs, N. (1982). *The troubled and troubling child.* San Francisco: Jossey-Bass.

Kazdin, A. (1985). *Treatment of antisocial behavior in children and adolescents.* Homewood, IL: Dorsey Press.

Spaccarelli, S., Cotler, S., & Penman, D. (1992). Problem-solving skills training as a supplement to behavioral parent training. *Cognitive Therapy and Research, 16,* 1-18.

Taylor, T. K., Schmidt, F., Pepler, D., & Hodgins, H. (1998). A comparison of eclectic treatment with Webster-Stratton's Parents and Children Series in a Children's Mental Health Center: A randomized controlled trial. *Behavior Therapy, 29,* 221-240.

Webster-Stratton, C. (1984). Randomized trial of two parent-training programs for families with conduct-disordered children. *Journal of Consulting and Clinical Psychology, 52,* 666-678.

Webster-Stratton, C. (1989). Systematic comparison of consumer satisfaction of three cost-effective parent training programs for conduct problem children. *Behavior Therapy, 20,* 103-115.

Webster-Stratton, C. (1990a). Enhancing the effectiveness of self-administered videotape parent training for families with conduct-problem children. *Journal of Abnormal Child Psychology, 18,* 479-492.

Webster-Stratton, C. (1990b). Long-term follow-up of families with young conduct problem children: From preschool to grade school. *Journal of Clinical Child Psychology, 19,* 144-149.

Webster-Stratton, C. (1998). Preventing conduct problems in Head Start children: Strengthening parent competencies. *Journal of Consulting and Clinical Psychology, 66,* 715-730.

Webster-Stratton, C., & Hammond, M. (1997). Treating children with early-onset conduct problems: A comparison of child and parent training interventions. *Journal of Consulting and Clinical Psychology, 65,* 93-109.

Webster-Stratton, C., & Hammond, M. (1998). Conduct problems and level of social competence in Head Start children: Prevalence, pervasiveness and associated risk factors. *Clinical Child Psychology and Family Psychology Review, 1,* 101-124.

Webster-Stratton, C., & Hancock, L. (1998). Parent training: Content, Methods and Processes. In E. Schaefer (Ed.), *Handbook of Parent Training, Second Edition* (pp. 98-152). New York: Wiley and Sons.

Webster-Stratton, C., Hollinsworth, T., & Kolpacoff, M. (1989). The long-term effectiveness and clinical significance of three cost-effective training programs for families with conduct-problem children. *Journal of Consulting and Clinical Psychology, 57,* 550-553.

Webster-Stratton, C., & Hooven, C. (1998). Parent training for child conduct problems. In T. Ollendick (Ed.), *Comprehensive clinical psychology* (pp. 186-219). Oxford, England: Elsevier Science.

Webster-Stratton, C., Kolpacoff, M., & Hollinsworth, T. (1988). Self-administered videotape therapy for families with conduct-problem children: Comparison with two cost-effective treatments and a control group. *Journal of Consulting and Clinical Psychology, 56,* 558-566.

Aggression Replacement Training: A Multimodal Intervention for Aggressive Adolescents

Linda A. Reddy, PhD
Arnold P. Goldstein, PhD

SUMMARY. This article provides an overview of Aggression Replacement Training (ART), an empirically validated and theoretically grounded multimodal intervention designed to prevent and reduce aggression in adolescents. ART consists of three components: (1) skills streaming, designed to teach a broad range of social skills; (2) anger control training, a method for empowering youth to modify their own anger responsiveness; and (3) moral reasoning education, training to motivate youth to use skills acquired through the other two training components. Implementation issues are presented. Strategies to successfully transfer and maintain acquired skills, as well as enhance trainee motivation, are outlined. Efficacy studies suggest that ART is an effective program for aggressive adolescents in a wide range of treatment settings. *[Article copies available for a fee from The Haworth Document Delivery Service: 1-800-342-9678. E-mail address: <getinfo@haworthpressinc.com> Website: <http://www.HaworthPress.com> © 2001 by The Haworth Press, Inc. All rights reserved.]*

KEYWORDS. Aggression replacement training, conduct problems, anger control

Linda A. Reddy, PhD, is affiliated with Fairleigh Dickinson University. Arnold P. Goldstein is affiliated with Syracuse University.

Address correspondence to: Linda A. Reddy, PhD, School Psychology Programs, Fairleigh Dickinson University, 1000 River Road, Teaneck, NJ 07666 (E-mail: Reddy@alpha.FDU.Edu).

Preparation for this manuscript was supported by grants 2-022627 and 2-022682 from the Society for the Study of School Psychology and a University Faculty Research Grant awarded to the first author.

[Haworth co-indexing entry note]: "Aggression Replacement Training: A Multimodal Intervention for Aggressive Adolescents." Reddy, Linda A., and Arnold P. Goldstein. Co-published simultaneously in *Residential Treatment for Children & Youth* (The Haworth Press, Inc.) Vol. 18, No. 3, 2001, pp. 47-62; and *Innovative Mental Health Interventions for Children: Programs That Work* (ed: Steven I. Pfeiffer, and Linda A. Reddy) The Haworth Press, Inc., 2001, pp. 47-62. Single or multiple copies of this article are available for a fee from The Haworth Document Delivery Service [1-800-342-9678, 9:00 a.m. - 5:00 p.m. (EST). E-mail address: getinfo@haworthpressinc.com].

MISSION AND GOALS OF ART

ART, a multimodal psychoeducational intervention, is designed to promote the social behavior of chronically aggressive adolescents. The underlying assumption of ART is aggressive behavior in adolescents is a multidimensional problem that is inhibited and/or fostered by a number of external (e.g., parents, peers, media) and internal factors (e.g., poor problem solving and social skills, primitive moral reasoning, impulsivity) in the environment. This complex problem, therefore, warrants a multilevel and multichannel approach to treatment. ART is a prescriptive and individualized approach that encompasses three treatment components that combine in their joint impact to reduce and prevent aggression in adolescents. Skills Streaming, the behavioral component of ART, is aimed at improving prosocial skills through modeling, role-playing, praise and performance feedback, and real-world activities in the home, school, and community. Anger Control Training (ACT), the emotional component of ART, is designed to provide adolescents ways to enhance their self-control when provocation is and is not present in social situations and help reduce the occurrence of anger responsiveness. Moral Reasoning Training, the values component of ART, focuses on increasing a youth's ability to respond prosocially when social events challenge or diminish control over impulsive anger and aggression. Training for all three components takes place on a weekly basis. ART can be easily implemented by trained teachers, counselors, child care workers, therapeutics foster care parents, and others who care for aggressive youngsters.

HISTORY AND DEVELOPMENT OF ART

As noted by this volume, increased aggression in American youth and public outcry have launched many initiatives to reduce and prevent the incidences of aggression in schools and communities. The ART program was developed, in part, from the rise in youth violence and the emergence of three important and related areas of research on aggression in children, Skill Streaming, ACT, and Moral Education.

Skill Streaming. Goldstein's Structured Learning Therapy, presently called Skill Streaming, was based on Bandura's (1973) social learning theory and behavior-deficit model and the psychological skills training movement of the 1970s. The Skill Streaming approach is a set of behavioral procedures designed to enhance prosocial skills in preschoolers (McGinnis & Goldstein, 1990), elementary school children (McGinnis & Goldstein, 1997), and adolescents (Goldstein & McGinnis, 1997).

Skill Streaming for adolescents is a systematic, psychoeducational intervention that encompasses a 50-skill curriculum of prosocial behaviors (Goldstein & McGinnis, 1997). The Skill Streaming curriculum is implemented in small groups of adolescents (i.e., six to eight) who share similar prosocial skill deficits. Teaching strategies used to foster learning include: (1) *modeling*–experts demonstrate behaviors and skills in which the adolescents are weak or lacking, (2) *role playing*–guided opportunities to practice and rehearse appropriate interpersonal behaviors, (3) *performance feedback*–adolescents are frequently praised and provided feedback on how well they model the experts' skills and behaviors, and (4) *generalization training*–adolescents are encouraged to engage in activities designed to enhance their use of learned skills in real-world situations. Skills learned from these teaching methods are clustered in six areas: (1) *beginning social skills* (e.g., starting a conversation, introducing yourself, giving a compliment), (2) *advanced social skills* (e.g., asking for help, giving instructions, apologizing), (3) *skills for dealing with feelings* (e.g., dealing with someone's anger, coping with sadness and fear, expressing affection to others), (4) *alternatives to aggression* (e.g., helping others, responding to teasing, keeping out of fights), (5) *skills for dealing with stress* (e.g., coping with being left out, preparing for a stressful conversation), and (6) *planning skills* (e.g., setting goals, setting priorities for solving problems). The effectiveness of Skill Streaming has been documented in over 12 investigations (Goldstein & McGinnis, 1997). In general, findings revealed that over 90 percent of aggressive children and adolescents trained in the program acquire the skills taught. However, findings indicated that the use of skills in natural settings (i.e., transfer of skills) was more limited. As a result, Goldstein and his colleagues (Goldstein, Glick, & Gibbs, 1998) incorporated two additional training components, ACT and Moral Education Training, to increase the acquisition and transfer of learned skills across settings.

Anger Control Training (ACT). Feindler, Marriott, and Iwata's (1984) ACT was partially based on Novaco's (1975) and Meichenbaum's (1977) seminal work on self instructional training for anger and stress inoculation approaches. The primary objective of ACT is to teach adolescents to control and better manage their anger. Skill Streaming teaches adolescents *what to do instead of aggression*, while ACT teaches adolescents *what not to do* in anger-instigating situations. Based on Novaco's self-instructional approach, Feindler outlined a sequence of behavioral chains for anger prevention. During ten sessions, adolescents are taught to deal with provocations ("daily hassles") by following a series of behavioral steps that identify: (1) *triggers*–external events and internal appraisals that serve as provocation to anger, (2) *cues*–physical and kinesthetic experiences that indicate the presence and arousal level of anger to the adolescent, (3) *reducers*–strategies that reduce the youth's level of anger further, such as deep breathing, imagery, and counting backwards, (4) *reminders*–use of self statement that further decreases anger arousal by disputing and replacing internal triggers, and (5) *self-evaluation*–technique to appraise how well the youth is implementing the previous steps. ACT is a multiple step process in which aggressive youth are also trained to perceive and interpret the behavior or intentions of those around them. Attention to external triggers and internal interpretations of these triggers in the environment is emphasized.

Skill Streaming and ACT provide youngsters knowledge and skills on "what to do" and "not to do" when social situations instigate aggression. However, children may still choose to act aggressively since aggression is often reinforced and/or encouraged in homes, schools, and/or communities. Training designed to enhance children's values and moral reasoning are critically important for the prevention of aggression (Goldstein, Glick, & Gibbs, 1998).

Moral Education Training. Based on the pioneer work of Kohlberg (1969, 1973), youngsters exposed to moral dilemmas, in a group context where children are reasoning at different levels, results in cognitive conflict. The resolution of cognitive conflicts frequently enhances children's moral reasoning to that of higher-level peers in the group. Although this has been consistently found, changes in moral behavior have been equivocal (e.g., Arbuthnot & Goldon, 1983; Zimmerman, 1983). It is postulated that aggressive children do not have the skills and behavior for inhibiting aggression and acting prosocially. Goldstein and his colleagues (Goldstein, Glick, & Gibbs, 1998) believe that Kohlberg's moral reasoning model in combination with Skill Streaming and ACT provides a comprehensive effective arsenal for reducing aggression in youth.

ART *AS A MULTICHANNEL APPROACH*

ART encompasses three unique and complementary training components that in combination yield reliable and long-term positive outcomes. Table 1 presents an example of a ten-week ART core curriculum. ART can be offered in a variety of lengths depending on the nature and severity of the children's deficits. Group members attend ART sessions three times a week, with one session each devoted to Skill Streaming, ACT, and/or Moral Reasoning Training. A session is typically 45 to 50 minutes, with Moral Reasoning Training lasting longer (i.e., up to 1.5 hours).

TRAINEE SELECTION AND PREPARATION

The ART program is designed for youngsters who exhibit substantial deficits in prosocial skills, anger control, and moral reasoning. In most cases, adolescents are assigned to the program by staff responsible for their education and well-being. Given the involuntary nature of some ART programs, special considerations for preparing and motivating trainees for the program are warranted. It is recommended that no more than six to eight trainees are assigned to a group. Fewer trainees (i.e., as few as two trainees) may be necessary and desirable if the trainees are very resistant and aggressive. As the group culture builds, an additional trainee may be added to the group per week.

Once groups are formed, trainers prepare and motivate trainees for the program. Program information such as the purpose, procedures, incentives, and group rules is presented first to each youth and then to the entire group. The purpose of ART is presented to each trainee. For example, a trainer may say, "Remember when you lost your privilege after fighting with John? These meetings will help you think and behave in ways that will help you not get into trouble." Such statements prepare and motivate youngsters for the program. General procedures are explained such as the group will meet three times a week, meetings will help trainees learn skill alternatives to aggres-

TABLE 1. Ten-Week ART Curriculum

Week	Skill Streaming	Moral Reasoning Training	Anger Control Training
1	Making a Complaint 1. Decide what your complaint is. 2. Decide whom to complain to. 3. Tell that person your complaint. 4. Tell that person what you would like done about the problem. 5. Ask how he/she feels about what you've said.	The used car The dope pusher Riots in public places	Introduction 1. Explain the goals and "sell it" to the youngsters. 2. Explain the rules for participating and the training procedures. 3. Give initial assessments of the ABCs of aggressive behavior: A = What led up to it? B = What did you do? C = What were the consequences? 4. Review goals, procedures, ABCs.
2	Understanding the Feelings of Others 1. Watch the other person 2. Listen to what the other person is saying. 3. Figure out what the person might be feeling. 4. Think about ways to show you understand what he/she is feeling. 5. Decide on the best way and do it.	The passenger ship The case of Charles Manson LSD	Triggers 1. Review the 1st session. 2. Introduce the Hassle Log. 3. Discuss what makes you feel angry (triggers). 4. Role-play triggers. 5. Review the Hassle Log and triggers.
3	Getting Ready for a Difficult Conversation 1. Think about how you will feel during the conversation. 2. Think about how the other person will feel. 3. Think about different ways you could say what you want to do. 4. Think about what the other person might say back to you 5. Think about any other things that might happen during the conversations. 6. Choose the best approach you can think of and try it.	Shoplifting Booby trap Plagiarism	Cues and Anger Reducers 1, 2, 3 1. Review the second session. 2. Discuss how to know when you are angry (cues). 3. Discuss what to do when you know you are angry. [Anger reducer 1: deep breathing] [Anger reducer 2: background counting] [Anger reducer 3: pleasant imagery] 4. Role-play triggers + cues + anger reducers. 5. Review the Hassle Log; trigger; cues; and anger reducers 1, 2, 3
4	Dealing with Someone Else's Anger 1. Listen to the person who is angry. 2. Try to understand what the angry person is saying and feeling. 3. Decide if you can say or do something to deal with the situation. 4. If you can, deal with the other person's anger.	Toy revolver Robin Hood case Drugs	Reminders 1. Review the 3rd session. 2. Introduce reminders. 3. Model using reminders. 4. Role-play triggers + cues + anger reducers + reminders. 5. Review reminders.
5	Keeping Out of Fights 1. Stop and think about why you want to fight. 2. Decide what you want to happen in the long run. 3. Think about other ways to handle the situation besides fighting. 4. Decide on the best way to handle the situation and do it.	Private country road New York versus Gerald Young Saving a life	Self-Evaluation 1. Review the 4th session. 2. Introduce self-evaluation. [self-rewarding; self-coaching] 3. Role-play triggers + cues + anger reducers + reminders + self-evaluation. Review self-evaluation.
6	Helping Others 1. Decide if the other person might need and want your help. 2. Think of ways you could be helpful. 3. Ask the other person if he/she needs and wants your help. 4. Help the other person.	The kidney transplant Bomb shelter Misrepresentation	Thinking Ahead (Anger Reducer 4) 1. Review the 5th session. 2. Introduce thinking ahead. [Short- and long-term consequences] [Internal and external consequences] 3. Role-play "if-then" thinking ahead. 4. Role-play triggers + cues + anger reducers + reminders + self-evaluation. 5. Review thinking ahead.

TABLE 1 (continued)

Week	Skill Streaming	Moral Reasoning Training	Anger Control Training
7	Dealing with an Accusation	Lt. Berg	Angry Behavior Cycle
	1. Think about what the other person has accused you of.	Perjury	1. Review the sixth session.
	2. Think about why the person might have accused you.	Doctor's responsibility	2. Introduce the Angry Behavior Cycle. [Identify your own anger-provoking behavior.] [Change your own anger-provoking behavior.]
	3. Think about ways to answer the person's accusation.		3. Role-play triggers + cues + anger reducer + reminders + self-evaluation.
	4. Choose the best way and do it.		4. Review the Angry Behavior Cycle.
8	Dealing with Group Pressure	Noisy child	Rehearsal of Full Sequence
	1. Think about what the group wants you to do and why.	The stolen car	1. Review the seventh session.
	2. Decide what you want to do.	Discrimination	2. Introduce the use of Skill Streaming skills in place of aggression.
	3. Decide how to tell the group what you want to do.		3. Role-playing triggers + cues + anger reducers + reminders + Skill Streaming skill + self-evaluation.
	4. Tell the group what you have decided.		
9	Expressing Affection	Defense of other persons	Rehearsal of Full Sequence
	1. Decide if you have good feelings about the other person.	Lying in order to help someone	1. Review the Hassle Logs.
	2. Decide if the person would like to know about your feelings.	Rockefeller's suggestion	2. Role-play triggers + cues + anger reducers + reminders + Skill Streaming skill + self-evaluation.
	3. Choose the best way to express your feelings.		
	4. Choose the best time and place to express your feelings.		
	5. Express your feelings in a friendly way.		
10	Responding to Failure	The desert	Overall Review
	1. Decide if you have failed at something.	The threat	1. Review the Hassle Logs.
	2. Think about why you failed.	Drunken driving	2. Recap anger control techniques.
	3. Think about what you could do to keep from failing another time.		3. Role-play triggers + cues + anger reducers + reminders + Skill Streaming skill + self-evaluation.
	4. Decide if you want to try again.		4. Give reinforcement for participation and encourage trainees to continue.
	5. Try again using your new idea.		

sion, ways to control their anger, and methods for solving problems more effectively. Incentives for participation are also outlined, as well as the rules that govern how they are earned or lost. Similar to other training programs, the core qualities of the group play an important role for success. The atmosphere of the group, whether it is a safe place, free from put-downs, bullying, etc. is critical. ART trainers function as competent teachers, models, and protectors. Trainers must be vigilant for behavior problems and responsive to correct any trainee's efforts to intimidate and bully other members. To enhance group participation, compliance, and motivation, trainees should be encouraged to participate fully in establishing their own group rules.

Rules pertaining to attendance, participation, confidentiality, management of disagreements, and other topics for the setting should be suggested. Additional strategies for enhancing trainee motivation and managing resistance are presented in Goldstein, Glick, and Gibbs (1998).

TRAINER SELECTION AND PREPARATION

Teachers, counselors, school psychologists, child care workers, and correctional officers are examples of persons who can serve as ART trainers. Effective trainers possess three related qualities: (1) ease with adolescents, individually and in groups, (2) competence in the use of behavior modification procedures, and (3) effective teaching skills for adolescents with diverse learning abilities and styles. Preparation of ART trainers follows an apprenticeship training sequence. Trainers-to-be first thoroughly review all the training manuals and materials. Attendance at one of the trainer preparation workshops can be used to augment the written materials. Trainers will then participate in mock Skill Streaming, ACT, and Moral Reasoning Training led by experienced trainers in which the trainer-to-be participates as a pretend adolescent trainee. Trainers will observe experienced trainers lead ART groups and then will serve as co-leaders with another experienced ART trainer. Finally, trainers are assigned to lead a group while an experienced trainer observes.

Skill Streaming Component of ART. As previously noted, the Skill Streaming component of ART consists of 50 skills, grouped into six skill categories. Each skill is broken down into its behavioral steps, which are modeled by the trainers and role-played by each adolescent during the session. Collectively the behavioral steps illustrate the implementation of the skill (e.g., "making a complaint" on Table 1).

Skill selection is critically important for designing an effective ART program. Skills may be selected based on the strengths and weaknesses of the group members. It is recommended that a multi-method and multi-source approach be used for assessing skill level. Assessment methods such as direct observation, interviews, trial groups, and Skill Streaming checklists are particularly helpful. Direct observation is especially valuable if the trainers who plan to lead the group are the same people (e.g., teachers, direct care staff) who care for the youngsters on a daily basis. In addition, Skill Streaming checklists, available in teacher, direct care staff, parent, and student versions, are valuable tools for skill selection.

Skill negotiation is a potentially powerful aspect of treatment that motivates and empowers group members for training. This can be accomplished by asking group members to complete a Skill Streaming checklist during the first session. Information gathered from the member-completed skill checklists, in part, could be used to select and prioritize many of the skills taught to the group. This consumer approach (i.e., "give the consumers what they want") has proven to be a powerful motivator for training.

A number of program operations need to be considered for successfully implementing the Skill Streaming component of ART. Program operations may include trainee selection, trainer collaboration, frequency of sessions, program length, and room arrangement and assembly of materials. Trainees may be assigned to ART groups based on their skill deficits and/or apparent need for improvement in interpersonal and/or anger management skills. If more than one group is offered, youngsters may be grouped with others who exhibit similar patterns of skill deficits and/or who share identical grouping elements (i.e., adolescents from the same class, living unit, neighborhood). Trainer collaboration is strongly recommended for implementing ART. Two trainers, one trainer leading the group and the second sitting in the group, provide an ideal training arrangement for simultaneously fostering skill development and managing disruptive and aggressive behavior during training. If two trainers are not possible, parents, teachers, and other adults should be used. The frequency of the training sessions are important given the intensity and multimodal nature of ART. In a 10-week ART program, Skill Streaming Training should take place no more than once a week to allow group members the time to practice skills in their daily lives. The length of an ART program can vary widely from the 10-week core curriculum to a more extensive training that takes place during the course of a year. Program length may also be defined by the number of skills taught and learned. The goal of ART is to teach skills that are not only learned, but also successfully used in a youngster's daily life. Therefore, trainers should not present new skills until previous skills have been fully acquired. Room arrangement and materials for ART Skill Streaming are inexpensive and readily available in schools and other facilities. Placing chairs in a horseshoe-shaped arrangement permits easy interaction among group members and trainers. Materials may include a copy of the ART training manual, a chalkboard or easel pad, a set of skill cards for each group member, and poster board to display skill steps in the training room. The ART training manual costs $25.95 and videotaped training workshop courses can be purchased for $495, including a set of six videotapes and 10 copies of workshop supplements. Skill cards (i.e., cost $25 for a set of 400 3 × 5 cards) are available as part of the Skill Streaming Adolescent Curriculum (Goldstein & McGinnis, 1997), however, hand-printed versions on index cards work well too.

As mentioned, training procedures used to foster learning include modeling, role-playing, performance feedback, and generalization training. To successfully implement the four training procedures, trainers lead the group through nine training steps: (1) define the skill, (2) model the skill, (3) establish trainee skill need, (4) select a role-player, (5) set up the role-play, (6) conduct the role-play, (7) provide performance feedback, (8) assign skill homework, and (9) select the next role-player. These training steps are used to define, reinforce, and generalize skill acquisition across settings. A detailed description of each training step is provided in Goldstein, Glick, and Gibbs (1998).

ACT Component of ART. ACT teaches trainees what not to do (i.e., be aggressive) and how not to do it (i.e., appropriate use of anger control techniques) during provocation. ACT consists of four implementation procedures–modeling, role-playing, performance feedback, and homework–that facilitate the administration of the curriculum. Trainers model the proper use of the anger reduction techniques, help trainees' practice of anger management steps (i.e., lead role-playing activities), provide trainees corrective feedback about how their practice matches the model, and encourage and monitor trainees' practice of skills outside of group through the use of homework.

Modeling begins when the trainer describes an anger control technique that will be demonstrated and a conflict situation in which the technique will be used. Ideally, two trainers are available to model the technique and act out the conflict situation. Once the scene is presented, the trainers summarize the technique used and discuss it with the group. Helpful guidelines for modeling include: (1) use at least two examples for each demonstration, (2) select scenes relevant to the trainees, (3) arrange that all scenes result in a positive outcome, and (4) portray the main actor as a person close to the trainees' age, verbal ability, socioeconomic background, etc.

After each presentation is modeled, trainees are asked to participate in role-plays to practice the modeled anger control techniques in situations the group recently experienced or expect to experience in the near future. General guidelines for role-playing include: (1) before beginning the role play, remind the trainees of their parts, (2) encourage the group members to carefully attend to whether the main actor is using the described anger management technique correctly, (3) if either actor deviates from their role, stop the scene and encourage the trainee to resume his/her role, (4) if the role play departs from the anger control technique, stop the role play, give instructions as needed, and restart the process, and (5) all trainees should have the opportunity to practice using the technique in a situation they have encountered or are about to encounter in the future.

After each role-play, group members briefly provide feedback to the actors on their performance. Feedback is provided as follows: actors are asked to share their reactions, observers are invited to comment on how well the technique was used, trainers comment on how well the technique was used, and the actors comment on the role-play and feedback they received. Guidelines for providing reinforcement include: (1) provide praise only after role-plays in which the technique was correctly used, (2) praise actors for their help and cooperation, (3) match the quality of the role-play with the praise given, (4) if the role-play departs significantly from what was intended, do not provide praise, and (5) praise trainees for improving their role-playing skills.

Weekly homework assignments require trainees to actively participate during and after training sessions are completed. Homework assignments are recorded on a "Hassle Log" which serves as a valuable source for problem situations to role-play. Hassle logs are available for readers and nonreaders. An overview of a 10-week ACT sequence is shown in Table 1 and a detailed description of each ACT training session is presented in Goldstein, Glick, and Gibbs (1998).

Moral Reasoning Training Component of ART. Moral Reasoning Training is fostered through a series of social decision making meetings. Group decision making meetings offer youngsters opportunities to enhance their value and social perspective taking through the resolution of a series of specific problem situations.

Prior to each meeting, trainees are provided copies of a problem situation and asked to provide their responses to the situation before the meeting. Trainers chart the responses, summarize the consensus among the group, and use the information to prepare for the meeting.

At the start of the session, the trainer facilitates the development of some group rules. The trainer next fosters sociomoral development through four phases: (1) introducing the problem situation, (2) cultivating mature morality, (3) remediating moral developmental delay, and (4) consolidating mature morality. At the completion of each training session, the trainer conducts a self-evaluation checklist that parallels the four phases. During Phase I, introduce the problem situation, the trainer highlights for the group what the problem situation is and how it relates to their lives. Questions and discussion are encouraged. Phase I typically last 15 minutes. Once the group understands the problem situation, Phase II, cultivate mature morality, begins. The trainer creates an atmosphere of mature morality by reinforcing trainees for making use of positive decisions and mature moral reasoning. Once a mature moral atmosphere is created in the group, the trainer then shifts the focus of the group on those individuals who exhibit moral developmental delays or limited social perspective taking skills (i.e., Phase III). This is accomplished by the trainer inviting the negative group members to explain their views, publicly record their reasons for their decision on an easel pad or chalkboard, and invite majority group members to respond. After mature morality has been cultivated and challenged, consolidation of mature morality (i.e., Phase IV) is accomplished. During Phase IV, the trainer seeks consensus among trainees for positive and mature decision making. During this process, trainees with initially immature moral judgement continue to feel pressure to reconsider and/or adjust their decision making. The Moral Reasoning Training component of ART often is appealing since the training encourages and reinforces autonomy and self direction and the situational content is highly relevant to the everyday lives of the trainees.

GENERALIZATION
AND MAINTENANCE OF PERFORMANCE

Several methods are used to encourage the generalizability and maintenance of skills learned during the program. Useful transfer-enhancing procedures include: (1) provision of general principles–the trainee thoroughly understands the principles underlying the skills taught and the situations the trainee encounters, (2) overlearning–correctly rehearse/practice skills learned over time, (3) stimulus variability-provide varied training experiences, (4) identical elements–trainees are trained in real-world locations (e.g., school, playground) with persons the trainees interact with on a daily basis, and (5) mediated generalization–instruct the trainee in a series of self-regulation competencies such as self-recording, self-reinforcement, self-punishment (i.e., response cost techniques), and self-instruction.

Behavioral techniques also can be used to increase the maintenance of skills acquired during the program. Maintenance-enhancing strategies that are particularly helpful include: (1) thinning of reinforcements, (2) delaying reinforcements, (3) fading prompts, (4) providing booster sessions, (5) preparing for nonreinforcement in the natural environment, (6) programming for reinforcement in the natural environment, and (7) identifying natural reinforcers. Generalization of skills is further promoted if trainees are concurrently taught a range of complementary skills. For this purpose, the Prepare Curriculum (Goldstein, 1988), an expansion of the ART model, provides a broad array of interpersonal, prosocial competencies for aggressive and skill-deficient youth.

OUTCOME EVALUATION

The efficacy of ART has been established in over 12 investigations (Goldstein, Glick & Gibbs, 1998). ART can be easily replicated and evaluated in treatment settings such as juvenile detention facilities, residential care, community-based programs, and schools. Three outcome studies are briefly presented to illustrate ART's effectiveness with aggressive youth from culturally diverse backgrounds.

The first evaluation study of ART was conducted with 60 male juveniles incarcerated at the Annsville Youth Center in New York, a limited-secure detention center (Goldstein & Glick, 1987). Most juveniles were at the Center for crimes such as unarmed robbery, burglary, and drug offenses. Subjects were assigned to one of three groups: (1) 10-week ART program, (2) no-ART brief instructions control group, and (3) a no-treatment control group. The brief instructions control group was included to control for the possibility that ART derived skill gains were not due to ART, but instead to subjects' enhanced motivation to display skills they already possessed. Results revealed that ART participants, compared to both control groups, significantly acquired and transferred four of the ten Skill Streaming skills. Acquired skills included expressing a complaint, responding to anger, dealing with group pressure, and preparing for a stressful conversation. Moreover, adolescents that participated in both control groups exhibited more and higher intensity acting out behavior than those that participated in ART. A one-year follow-up study was also conducted to further determine the transfer effects of ART on adolescents' community functioning after discharge from the center. Among the 54 juveniles released, seventeen participated in ART, and 37 did not. Parole officers were asked to complete a global community functioning measure on each juvenile. ART youth were rated with significantly higher community functioning in the areas of home, family, peer, and legal than youth that did not receive ART.

Goldstein and Glick (1989) replicated the Annsville investigation with 51 juvenile delinquents in MacCormick Youth Center in New York, a maximum-security facility for youth that have committed violent crimes such as rape, murder, and manslaughter. Subjects were assigned to one of the three previously mentioned groups. Consistent with the Annsville study, the ART group significantly learned and transferred more skill streaming skills (i.e., five of the ten skills) than the two control groups. In contrast to the Annsville study, ART juveniles displayed greater improvements in moral reasoning than the two control groups. Improvements in prosocial behaviors such as offering or accepting criticism appropriately, using self-control when provoked, and reductions in impulsivity were found among ART youth. However, no group differences were found in the number and intensity of acting out behaviors. Since the MacCormick Center is a well-staffed locked facility that operates under a tighter system of sanctions and control than the Annsville Center, opportunities for acting-out are possibly reduced for all three groups in this study.

Given the positive results from the two investigations with incarcerated youth, Goldstein and his colleagues (Goldstein, Glick, Irwin, McCartney, & Rubama, 1989) conducted a larger community-based investigation examining the impact of ART and parent training on juveniles' community functioning. The community-based study included 84 adolescents previously released from juvenile detention. Participants were assigned to one of the three conditions: (1) ART provided to adolescents and their parents, (2) ART provided to adolescents, and (3) no-ART control. The ART program was offered for three months, meetings were scheduled twice a week, for a total of 25 sessions. Each session lasted approximately 90 minutes. An ART session was provided to parents and family members in condition 1 once a week. Home-based training was provided to those parents who could not attend the weekly meetings. Adolescents in the two ART conditions did not differ significantly from each other, however, they did differ significantly in their overall interpersonal skill competence than those in the no-ART control condition. Moreover, adolescents in both ART conditions reported feeling significantly less angry than the controls.

Based on these three investigations, as well as a number of subsequent ART efficacy evaluations (see Goldstein, Glick, & Gibbs, 1998), ART appears to be a multimodal intervention with considerable potential for reducing and preventing aggression in adolescents. Additionally, ART is a flexible cost effective program that can be easily transported and replicated in a wide variety of treatment settings.

REFERENCES

Arbuthnot, J., & Gordon, D.A. (1983). Moral reasoning development in correctional intervention. *Journal of Correctional Education, 34,* 133-138.

Bandura, A. (1973). *Aggression: A social learning analysis.* Englewood Cliffs, NJ: Prentice-Hall.

Feindler, E.L., Marriott, S.A., & Iwata, M. (1984). Group anger control training for junior high delinquents. *Cognitive Therapy and Research, 8,* 299-311.

Goldstein, A. P. (1973). *Structured learning therapy: Toward a psychotherapy for the poor.* New York: Academic.

Goldstein, A.P. (1988). *The prepare curriculum: Teaching prosocial competencies.* Champaign, IL: Research Press.

Goldstein, A.P., & Glick, B. (1987). *Aggression replacement training: A comprehensive intervention for aggressive youth.* Champaign, IL: Research Press.

Goldstein, A.P., Glick, B., & Gibbs, J. C. (1998). *Aggression replacement training: A comprehensive intervention for aggressive youth (rev. ed.).* Champaign, IL: Research Press.

Goldstein, A.P., Glick, B., Irwin, M.J., Pask, C., & Rubama, I. (1989). *Reducing delinquency: Intervention in the community.* New York: Pergamon Press.

Goldstein, A.P., & McGinnis, E. (1997). *Skillstreaming the adolescent: New strategies and perspectives for teaching prosocial skills (rev. ed.).* Champaign, IL: Research Press.

Kohlberg, L. (1969). Stage and sequence: The cognitive-developmental approach to socialization. In D.A. Goslin (Ed.), *Handbook of socialization theory and research.* Chicago: Rand McNally.

Kohlberg, L. (1973). *Collected papers on moral development and moral education.* Cambridge, MA: Harvard University, Center for Moral Education.

McGinnis, E., & Goldstein, A.P. (1990). *Skillstreaming in early childhood: Teaching prosocial skills to the preschool and kindergarten child.* Champaign, IL: Research Press.

McGinnis, E., & Goldstein, A.P. (1997). *Skillstreaming the elementary school child: New strategies and perspectives for teaching prosocial skills (rev. ed.).* Champaign, IL: Research Press.

Meichenbaum, D. (1977). *Cognitive behavior modification: An integrative approach.* New York: Plenum.

Novaco, R.W. (1975). *Anger control: The development and evaluation of an experimental treatment.* Lexington, MA: Lexington Books.

Zimmerman, D. (1983). Moral education. In Center for Research on Aggression (Ed.), *Prevention and control of aggression.* Elmsford, NY: Pergamon.

The Anger Coping Program:
An Empirically-Supported Treatment
for Aggressive Children

John E. Lochman, PhD
John F. Curry, PhD
Heather Dane, MA
Mesha Ellis, MA

SUMMARY. This article provides a history and overview of an Anger Coping Program for children with a history of aggressive behavior problems. The Anger Coping Program is a cognitive-behavioral intervention, which addresses the social-cognitive distortions and deficits of aggressive children. The structure and content of the program are briefly reviewed, and its application in residential treatment facilities is discussed. The dissemination of the program is discussed, and the results of outcome research on the Anger Coping Program are presented. The program has produced significant post-intervention improvements in children's behavior and social-cognitive processes. *[Article copies available for a fee from The Haworth Document Delivery Service: 1-800-342-9678. E-mail address: <getinfo@haworthpressinc.com> Website: <http://www.HaworthPress. com> © 2001 by The Haworth Press, Inc. All rights reserved.]*

John E. Lochman, PhD, Heather Dane, MA, and Mesha Ellis, MA, are all affiliated with The University of Alabama. John F. Curry, PhD, is affiliated with Duke University Medical Center.

The preparation of this article was supported by grants from the National Institute of Drug Abuse, and from the Center for Substance Abuse Prevention, Substance Abuse and Mental Health Services Administration.

Address correspondence to: John E. Lochman, PhD, Department of Psychology, Box 870348, The University of Alabama, Tuscaloosa, AL 35487.

[Haworth co-indexing entry note]: "The Anger Coping Program: An Empirically-Supported Treatment for Aggressive Children." Lochman, John E. et al. Co-published simultaneously in *Residential Treatment for Children & Youth* (The Haworth Press, Inc.) Vol. 18, No. 3, 2001, pp. 63-73; and: *Innovative Mental Health Interventions for Children: Programs That Work* (ed: Steven I. Pfeiffer, and Linda A. Reddy) The Haworth Press, Inc., 2001, pp. 63-73. Single or multiple copies of this article are available for a fee from The Haworth Document Delivery Service [1-800-342-9678, 9:00 a.m. - 5:00 p.m. (EST). E-mail address: getinfo@haworthpressinc.com].

KEYWORDS. Anger coping program, aggression, conduct problems

HISTORY AND OBJECTIVES
OF THE ANGER COPING PROGRAM

Given the detrimental and enduring effects of aggressive behavior in children, including harm to others and risk for future legal or mental health problems (Robins, 1978), there has been a significant effort to develop effective intervention programs to address aggression early in development. One such program is the Anger Coping program, developed by Lochman and his colleagues.

The Anger Coping program is an 18-session cognitive-behavioral intervention based in part on Dodge's information processing model (Dodge, 1993) as applied to aggressive children. According to this model, aggressive children have difficulties encoding social cues, accurately interpreting social events, generating multiple adaptive solutions to problems encountered, considering consequences of solutions and using this information to determine the best solution, and skillfully carrying out the solution once chosen (Lochman & Lenhart, 1993). Aggressive children attend to a narrower range of social cues, selectively attend to hostile cues, and perceive hostile intent in ambiguous situations. Highly aggressive children generate fewer social problem solutions overall and a higher proportion of physically aggressive solutions than other children (Lochman, Lampron, Burch, & Curry, 1985).

In accordance with these findings, the Anger Coping program was designed to improve the social-cognitive skills of aggressive children. The program began as a 12-session anger control program (Lochman, Nelson, & Sims, 1981), and has developed, because of ongoing intervention research findings, into the 18-session Anger Coping program. The mission of the Anger Coping program is to help aggressive children develop better perspective-taking skills, increase their awareness of the physiological signs of anger, improve social problem-solving skills, and increase their inventory of responses to problem situations (Lochman & Lenhart, 1993). Emphasis is placed on teaching skills in such a way that the children will be more likely to apply what they have learned in the outside world. Repetition, active participation, discussion, and role playing are all modes utilized to engage the children.

Adaptation to residential settings. Although originally designed for elementary-aged aggressive boys in a school setting, the Anger Coping program may be altered for use with girls, with older or younger children, or in a clinic setting. Another potential area of adaptation of the program is to modify it for the residential setting. From a practical standpoint, the Anger Coping program may be useful in a residential setting because of its ability to involve multiple children through a group format and because staff at different levels can be trained in the successful application of the program. Although its efficacy has not been formally evaluated in a residential setting, adaptation of the Anger Coping program to this environment appears promising.

KEY INGREDIENTS IN ANGER COPING TREATMENT

Typically, Anger Coping is delivered in a group format with two co-therapists. Groups of aggressive or impulsive boys present management challenges, which call for some degree of clinical experience and shared leadership responsibilities. At least one therapist must have experience with aggressive or oppositional children. It is optimal if one leader has training in group psychotherapy or group interventions (so that development of group norms can be monitored) and one has familiarity with the children's social setting. In our studies within the Durham, NC public school system, one therapist was typically a mental health professional and the other was a school guidance counselor.

Anger Coping groups require a behavioral contingency system for within-group behavior and a weekly goals system for time between sessions. A point system, for example, can be used, in which participants earn points for cooperative involvement in sessions, and lose points for disruptive or distracting behavior. Either individual or group rewards, such as snacks, ice cream, or other privileges, can be earned.

The required space and equipment needed to conduct Anger Coping groups are described below. Therapists will need stimulus cards or pictures involving social interactions to evoke individual responses to ambiguous situations. Therapists will likewise need an audio tape recorder with microphone, and equipment for taping and showing the children's final videotape group project.

A full description of the content of the 18-session Anger Coping program can be found in Lochman, FitzGerald and Whidby (1999) and Lochman, Lampron, Gemmer, and Harris (1987). A summary is included here. Each session has a set of objectives, although it may be necessary to carry over an objective from one session to the next.

The First Session focuses on helping the children to understand the purpose of the group, establishing group rules, introducing members to one another, and introducing the notion of individual differences in perceptions. Members can be asked to share examples of their own difficulties with anger control and they should be engaged in the process of formulating rules (confidentiality, disruptive behavior). The rules should be written on newsprint or a similar product for display in subsequent sessions. The Second Session introduces Goal-Setting. Teachers, or in a residential treatment setting, other program staff, are asked to assist by monitoring the child's goals on a daily basis. Within the group, the children are helped to articulate concrete, observable weekly goals.

The Third and Fourth Sessions focus on the role of thought in the control of emotions. "Practicing self-control" games are recommended to model and to evoke attentional control mechanisms and self-statements that enhance emotion regulation. Sessions Five and Six establish the notion of perspective-taking. Responses to stimulus cards are used to elicit varying perceptions of "what is happening in the picture." Perceptual and cognitive flexibility is encouraged by asking each member to give a different response.

Session Seven includes two key concepts. First, children are taught to identify their own physiological cues or bodily reactions signaling anger. Second, the impact of self-statements that enhance or diminish angry feelings is explored. Sessions Eight, Nine, and Ten present the problem-solving model that is integral to Anger Coping. Notions of defining a problem as such, of generating all possible alternative solutions, and of evaluating these possible solutions are introduced, discussed, and applied.

Sessions Eleven, Twelve, and Thirteen are devoted to the major group project, creating their own videotape demonstrating use of the Anger Coping, problem-solving method. The members write the script by identifying anger-arousing problems in the school (or residential) setting, generating possible solutions and consequences, and choosing one such problem to videotape. The final sessions (Fourteen to Eighteen) are then focused on applications of the model to additional problems the children want to solve. More videotapes may be made. The Goals, which will have been monitored and reinforced in each session, may serve as the focus of additional problem-solving work.

Anticipation of future challenges to anger control is included, and steps identified that are likely to help resolve such problems.

PROGRAM IMPLEMENTATION

In determining how to implement Anger Coping in a residential setting, one has to consider the basic structure of the program, training requirements, staffing and space needs, as well as the financial commitment. In terms of basic structure, the Anger Coping Program is quite amenable to residential settings because, like similar cognitive-behavioral programs, it provides manualized yet flexible treatment options for clinicians (Lochman, FitzGerald, & Whidby, 1999). Although group leaders are given guidelines for session planning, they are encouraged to individualize the sessions to meet the treatment needs of participants.

Although program participants generally meet once per week over the course of 18 sessions, the time commitment can be reduced to the original duration of 12 sessions. The program also has the capability of being expanded to 33 sessions, which allows the therapist(s) to explore more topics and teach a wider range of coping skills. The expanded version of the program, called the Coping Power Program (Lochman & Wells, 1996), includes group sessions and individual therapy for participants as well as parent training and teacher consultations. Because of the flexibility that is allowed through the Anger Coping Program, residential treatment planners should be careful to consider the time and space commitment needed in order for the program to work optimally.

The Anger Coping Program has been found to be most effective in the context of group therapy with sessions ranging between one hour and one and one-half hours. Group therapy allows participants to learn skills through a variety of modalities. Perhaps the most important modality is peer group interaction and feedback. Research suggests that a small, closed group, comprised of 5-7 children, provides the most conducive environment for participants to gain from the program (Lochman et al., 1999).

As noted above, two co-therapists are recommended. If a school campus is located on the grounds of the residential facility, teachers or school counselors are strongly encouraged to act as one co-leader. All lead therapists should have a Masters Degree or Doctorate in psychology, social work, counseling, or psychiatry. They should also have experience working with aggressive and behaviorally difficult children.

Intensive Anger Coping Program training typically consists of three full days of workshop sessions, monthly follow-up workshops, telephone consultations, and weekly session planning meetings. Group co-leaders should also take time to create and periodically reevaluate a group behavior-contingency program that outlines specific rewards and response costs for participants. Furthermore, because of the extreme behavioral difficulties that often accompany children enrolled in residential facilities, it is recommended that a behavioral aid attend group sessions in order to help with the behavioral management of participants.

When planning a residentially-based intervention, clinicians should be aware that the Anger Coping program has been found to be most effective when the groups are comprised of same-sex children with similar behavioral difficulties. When selecting participants, planners should recruit participants who are aware that their aggressive behavior not only is a nuisance to others but is also problematic for themselves. Consequently, a general assessment of potential group members is suggested to help clinicians select group members and customize the program to the needs of participants. The basic assessment should consist of a semi-structured interview with the child as well as self-report cognitive and behavioral rating scales.

Because many aggressive children are highly distractible, it is imperative for the group sessions to be held in a room with few visual, tactile, and auditory distractions. The therapy room should also have enough chairs for group participants and the group leaders to sit comfortably and be large enough to allow for the use of a poster board, chalkboard, or a dry-erase board. Because of the unpredictable nature of children with behavioral difficulties, the residential facility should have space for a "time-out" area that allows for the removal of disruptive participants from the group.

Due to limited resources, program planners may find themselves restricted within the residential setting regarding available staff and space. Consequently, the Anger Coping Program allows clinicians to work with residents individually and this has been found to be effective in teaching problem solving skills (Lochman et al., 1999).

The budget for implementing the Anger Coping Program in a residential setting should reflect wages for the group co-leaders and behavioral aids. If a parent training component is established, program planners may maximize parent attendance through snacks at meetings, arrangement for transportation, and provision of child care during the meetings. Program planners should also allow for the purchase of rewards, tokens, toys, and session materials for group or individual therapy participants. Session materials will include boards and pictures, record keeping materials, audio and video tape recorders and tapes, playing cards, games, puppets, and photocopying costs.

REPLICATION AND TRANSPORTABILITY

The intervention research that has been conducted on the Anger Coping Program has occurred in a series of randomized clinical trials conducted in the public school system in Durham, NC, over a 10-year period. Because of the significant improvements found in these studies, a task force of the American Psychological Association has identified the Anger Coping Program as one of the ten probably efficacious treatments for child and adolescent conduct problems (Brestan & Eyberg, 1998). As a result, a workshop on the Anger Coping program was presented at The Niagara Conference on Evidence-Based Treatments for Childhood Mental Health Problems in the summer of 1999. Over the past 20 years a number of similar workshops have been provided nationally on the Anger Coping Program to mental health clinicians, school counselors and school psychologists, and juvenile corrections staff. Successful large-scale implementations of the program have taken place in school systems in several counties, including Wake and Guilford counties in North Carolina. In the Wake County implementation, groups in 40 schools were conducted with over 200 children, and a local program evaluation found that children who had been in the program had reduced levels of aggressive behavior, improved problem-solving skills and improved academic achievement following their involvement in the program. These dissemination efforts have suggested that local staff in agencies and schools can usefully implement the Anger Coping program.

Grant-funded intervention research is currently being conducted on an expanded version of the Anger Coping Program. This expanded version is the Coping Power Program, which consists of a 33-session group intervention for children and a 16-session parent group intervention (Lochman & Wells, 1996). This program is typically offered over a

15 to 18 month period of time, and is particularly directed towards children making the transition from elementary to middle school. This program has been adapted for clinical research in several residential facilities, including a child psychiatry facility in the Netherlands, and a residential school for the deaf in North Carolina, indicating that these programs can be effectively used in residential settings.

In the course of these dissemination efforts, we have had to attend to the language and cultural appropriateness of the intervention, including adjusting the program to be relevant for children and families in other countries and with children who have unique communication difficulties because of a physical handicap. The curriculum and the program delivery system have been designed to be responsive to cultural and ethnic differences (e.g., African-American vs. European-American) in four ways. First, the literature about ethnic factors which influence social-cognitive processes and parenting processes, the targets of our intervention, was carefully reviewed. Second, we involve our African-American staff very actively in the development of our interventions, and they had a major impact on how we attempt to deliver our interventions. For example, through their input, we have relied less on videotape modeling of skills and more on the group leaders providing live modeling of competent and incompetent social skills. Third, rather than using a strict didactic approach in our groups, we actively have participants discuss what they do already that sometimes works, and we then use their examples to illustrate positive coping methods. We use a problem-solving approach to intervention, where we act as collaborative coaches rather than as teachers. Fourth, in our research we examine whether ethnic status influences the strength of intervention effects. In our research on these and other similar programs, we have found these forms of child and parent interventions to be similarly effective with African-American and European-American children and parents (Conduct Problems Prevention Research Group, 1999).

PROGRAM EVALUATION AND OUTCOMES

A thorough assessment of children's aggressive behavior and of the social-cognitive factors associated with their aggression is an extremely important part of designing a comprehensive treatment plan, and is critical for program evaluation efforts. In our intervention research and in our clinical assessments, we include a battery of behavioral and social-cognitive measures that is described in detail elsewhere (Lochman, Whidby & FitzGerald, in press). The core battery includes: (a) a behavior rating scale completed by the parents and if possible by the teachers; (b) a social problem-solving measure to assess children's rates and types of solutions generated; and (c) a measure of children's distorted encoding skills or their distorted attributions. Other assessment measures can include a structured interview, peer reports of children's behavior, measures of children's social goals, emotional understanding and empathy.

Research on the Anger Coping Program has indicated its effects on children's behavior by the end of intervention. In comparison with randomly assigned minimal treatment and untreated control conditions, Lochman, Burch, Curry and Lampron (1984) found that treated aggressive elementary school boys had reductions in independently observed disruptive-aggressive off-task behavior, reductions in parents' ratings of aggression, and improvements in self-esteem. Boys in the Anger Coping Program in this study who had the greatest reductions in aggressive behavior were boys who were initially the poorest problem solvers (Lochman, Lampron, Burch & Curry, 1985). In addition, better outcomes tended to occur for boys with more initial anxiety and somatization, and lower social acceptance from peers, suggesting that boys may have been more motivated for treatment because of a desire to decrease peer rejection and worries about the consequences resulting from their aggressive behavior. The post-treatment behavioral improvements in this study were replicated in subsequent studies (Lochman & Curry, 1986). At a three-year follow-up Anger Coping boys were found to have better problem-solving skills, self-esteem gains, and lower levels of substance use than an untreated control condition (Lochman, 1992). On these measures, the treated boys were in the same range as nonaggressive boys, indicating notable prevention effects on early substance use at the follow-up when boys were age 15. However, continued reduction in off-task behavior at school and in parents' ratings of aggression were only evident for treated boys who had received a brief booster treatment for themselves and their parents in a second school year. Thus, booster treatments with children and their parents may be critical for the maintenance of behavioral gains following this cognitive-behavioral Anger Coping Program.

Based on these findings, the multicomponent Coping Power intervention, which is an extension of the Anger Coping Program, is being evaluated in two randomized, controlled intervention trials. The series of programmatic research studies reviewed above have indicated that the Anger Coping and Coping Power Programs are promising, effective intervention methods for children who have had a history of aggressive behavior.

REFERENCES

Brestan, E.V. & Eyberg, S.M. (1998). Effective psychosocial treatments of conduct-disordered children and adolescents: 29 years, 82 studies, and 5,272 kids. *Journal of Clinical Child Psychology, 27,* 180-189.

Conduct Problems Prevention Research Group (1999). Initial impact of the Fast Track prevention trial for conduct problems: I. The high-risk sample. *Journal of Consulting and Clinical Psychology, 67,* 631-647.

Dodge, K. A. (1993). Social cognitive mechanisms in the development of conduct disorder and depression. *Annual Review of Psychology, 44,* 559-584.

Lochman, J.E. (1992). Cognitive-behavioral intervention with aggressive boys: Three-year follow-up and preventive effects. *Journal of Consulting and Clinical Psychology, 60,* 426-432.

Lochman, J.E., Burch, P.R., Curry, J.F., & Lampron, L.B. (1984). Treatment and generalization effects of cognitive-behavioral and goal-setting interventions with aggressive boys. *Journal of Consulting and Clinical Psychology, 52,* 915-916.

Lochman, J.E. & Curry, J.F. (1986). Effects of social problem-solving training and self-instruction training with aggressive boys. *Journal of Clinical Child Psychology, 15,*159-164.

Lochman, J.E., FitzGerald, D.P., & Whidby, J.M. (1999). Anger management with aggressive children. In C.E. Schaefer (Ed.), *Short-term psychotherapy groups for children* (pp. 301-349). Northvale, NJ: Jason Aronson.

Lochman, J.E., Lampron, L.B., Burch, P.R., & Curry, J.F. (1985). Client characteristics associated with behavior change for treated and untreated boys. *Journal of Abnormal Child Psychology, 13,* 527-538.

Lochman, J. E., Lampron, L. B., Gemmer, T. C., & Harris, S. R. (1987). Anger coping intervention with aggressive children: A guide to implementation in school settings. In P. A. Keller & S. R. Heyman (Eds.), *Innovations in clinical practice: A source book* (Vol. 6, pp. 339-356). Sarasota, FL: Professional Resource Exchange.

Lochman, J. E., & Lenhart, L. A. (1993). Anger Coping intervention for aggressive children: Conceptual models and outcome effects. *Clinical Psychology Review, 13,* 785-805.

Lochman, J. E., Nelson, W. M., & Sims, J. P. (1981). A cognitive behavioral program for use with aggressive children. *Journal of Clinical Child Psychology, 10,* 146-148.

Lochman, J.E. & Wells, K.C. (1996). A social-cognitive intervention with aggressive children: Prevention effects and contextual implementation issues. In R. Dev. Peters & R. J. McMahon (Eds.), *Prevention and early intervention: Childhood disorders, substance use, and delinquency* (pp. 111-143). Newbury Park, CA: Sage.

Lochman, J.E., Whidby, J.M., & FitzGerald, D.P. (in press). Cognitive-behavioral assessment and treatment with aggressive children. In P. Kendall (Ed.), *Child and adolescent therapy,* Second Edition. New York: Guilford.

Robins, L. N. (1978). Sturdy childhood predictors of adult antisocial behaviour: Replications from longitudinal studies. *Psychological Medicine, 8,* 611-622.

Multisystemic Therapy

Scott W. Henggeler, PhD

SUMMARY. This article provides an overview of multisystemic therapy (MST). Specifically, the theoretical and empirical foundations for the demonstrated clinical and cost effectiveness of MST in treating children and adolescents presenting serious clinical problems and their families are discussed. Key foundations include attention to the multi-determined nature of serious clinical problems, provision of services with high ecological validity, and use of intensive quality assurance mechanisms to support program fidelity. Issues pertaining to the successful transport of MST programs at clinical, organizational, and community levels also are highlighted. *[Article copies available for a fee from The Haworth Document Delivery Service: 1-800-342-9678. E-mail address: <getinfo@haworthpressinc.com> Website: <http://www.HaworthPress.com> © 2001 by The Haworth Press, Inc. All rights reserved.]*

KEYWORDS. Multisystemic therapy, high risk youth, serious emotional disturbance

Multisystemic therapy (MST; Henggeler, Schoenwald, Borduin, Rowland, & Cunningham, 1998) is an intensive family-based treatment for children and adolescents presenting serious clinical prob-

Scott W. Henggeler, PhD, is affiliated with the Family Services Research Center, Medical University of South Carolina.

Address correspondence to: Scott W. Henggeler, PhD, Family Services Research Center, Department of Psychiatry and Behavioral Sciences, Medical University of South Carolina, 67 President Street-Suite CPP, P.O. Box 250861, Charleston, SC 29451 (E-mail: henggesw@musc.edu).

Preparation of this manuscript was supported by grants MH51852 and MH59138 from the NIMH, AA122202 from NIAAA, DA10079 and DA-99-008 from NIDA, and 96.2013 from The Annie E. Casey Foundation.

[Haworth co-indexing entry note]: "Multisystemic Therapy." Henggeler, Scott W. Co-published simultaneously in *Residential Treatment for Children & Youth* (The Haworth Press, Inc.) Vol. 18, No. 3, 2001, pp. 75-85; and: *Innovative Mental Health Interventions for Children: Programs That Work* (ed: Steven I. Pfeiffer, and Linda A. Reddy) The Haworth Press, Inc., 2001, pp. 75-85. Single or multiple copies of this article are available for a fee from The Haworth Document Delivery Service [1-800-342-9678, 9:00 a.m. - 5:00 p.m. (EST). E-mail address: getinfo@haworthpressinc.com].

lems. The key underlying theoretical assumption of MST is that emotional and behavior problems are best understood when examined within the context of children's social environment. Consistent with Bronfenbrenner's (1979) theory of social ecology, behavior is viewed as influenced bidirectionally by the nature of one's relations with key social systems as well as the interactions among these systems. In the case of a child, these systems include the family, peer group, school, neighborhood, and social support context. Importantly, the view that behavior is multi-determined from factors across the youths' social ecology is strongly supported by decades of correlational and longitudinal research in the area of externalizing problems (Loeber & Hay, 1997) and similar evidence is emerging for internalizing problems such as depression (Birmaher, Ryan, Williamson, Brent, & Kaufman, 1996).

If behavior is multidetermined, as the research suggests, then to optimize the probability of favorable clinical outcomes, effective interventions must have the capacity to address a broad range of potential contributing factors across individual, family, peer, school, and community systems. The development of MST in the late 1970s was predicated on this notion, and findings from eight published randomized trials support the effectiveness of MST with youth presenting serious clinical problems and their families (Henggeler, 1999a). Moreover, MST has been identified as a highly promising treatment model by reviewers in the fields of substance abuse (e.g., McBride, Vander-Waal, VanBuren, & Terry, 1997; Stanton & Shadish, 1997), adolescent violence (e.g., Elliott, 1998; Tate, Reppucci, & Mulvey, 1995), and mental health (e.g., Kazdin & Weisz, 1998).

KEY TREATMENT INGREDIENTS

As described recently (Henggeler, 1999b), several key ingredients most likely account for the bases of the capacity of MST to achieve favorable outcomes with challenging clinical populations and to serve as a community-based alternative to out-of-home placements.

Comprehensive services. Although decades of research have shown that serious clinical problems are multidetermined (i.e., influenced by youth cognitive variables and skills, family relations, peer interactions, school variables, family support networks, and neighborhood context), prevailing mental health, juvenile justice, and drug abuse services address only a small subset of these factors, often in ways that increase problems (e.g., placing antisocial youths together in treatment). MST provides a comprehensive evaluation of risk and protective factors across the youth's and family's social ecology to determine the pertinent contributors to the identified problems. Then, individualized strategies are developed to address these determinants.

Ecologically valid. MST services are provided in home, school, and community settings to maximize ecological validity. Providing home-based services overcomes most barriers to service access, provides more valid clinical assessment and outcome information, and helps to engage the family in treatment. In addition, issues of treatment generalization are less pertinent because the clinical changes are occurring where the problems are evidenced (i.e., in home, school, and neighborhood settings). Finally, such intensive services are cost effective if out-of-home placements are prevented.

Quality assurance. In light of the established associations between fidelity to the MST treatment principles and youth outcomes (Henggeler, Melton, Brondino, Scherer & Hanley, 1997; Henggeler, Pickrel, & Brondino, 1999; Huey, Henggeler, Brondino, & Pickrel, in press), MST programs have intensive quality assurance protocols. MST on-site group supervision occurs at least weekly and follows a specified protocol (Henggeler & Schoenwald, 1998) that is outcome oriented. For MST dissemination sites, an MST consultant also provides weekly feedback following a specified protocol (Schoenwald, 1998) aimed at enhancing treatment fidelity and achieving outcomes. In addition, the consultant helps agencies address any organizational barriers to achieving program success. For both research and dissemination sites, standardized measures of caregiver ratings of treatment adherence are assessed every 6 weeks through an Internet information system (www. mstinstitute.org), and research sites include ratings by an MST expert of audiotaped treatment sessions for each clinician. Together, these procedures aim to optimize outcomes through promoting therapist adherence to MST.

Evidence-based interventions. The specific intervention strategies used within MST are familiar to most clinicians. MST clinicians use evidence-based intervention models such as the behavior therapies, cognitive behavior therapy, and the pragmatic family therapies. These interventions, however, are used within a social ecological conceptual framework and within a program philosophy that emphasizes accountability of providers for engagement and outcome, and commitment to removing barriers to service access.

Empowering caregivers. A fundamental assumption of MST is that the youth's caregiver is the key to favorable long-term outcomes, even if that caregiver presents serious clinical challenges. Hence, treatment goals are defined by caregivers, and the majority of MST clinical resources are devoted to developing the capacity of the caregiver to achieve those goals (versus treating the youth individually). The MST analytic process (Henggeler, Schoenwald et al., 1998) is used to delineate barriers to effective parenting (e.g., drug abuse, mental illness, low social support), and to develop strategies to address these barriers. Hence, MST programs must have considerable expertise in evidence-based services for serious adult psychopathology.

Accountability. MST programs are accountable for engaging families in treatment and for achieving favorable youth and family outcomes. High accountability requires access to the resources needed to be effective (e.g., relatively high salary, low caseloads, strong clinical support, organizational support), and assumes that clinicians will benefit from program success and be provided opportunities to enhance their skills when individual success rates are low.

PROGRAM STRUCTURE

Comprehensive descriptions of MST clinical procedures, outcomes, and program structure are provided in Henggeler, Schoenwald et al. (1998) and Henggeler, Rone, Thomas, and Timmons-Mitchell (1998). This section briefly describes MST program structure.

Needs assessment. MST programs are most appropriate in communities where stakeholders across the service systems (i.e., juvenile justice, mental health, social welfare, schools, family court) and funders are concerned with improving youth and family outcomes and/or decreasing rates of out-of-home placement. An early step after the articulation of such goals by community stakeholders is the initiation of contact with MST Services, Inc. (268 W. Coleman Blvd., Suite 2E, Mount Pleasant, SC 29464; <keller@mstservices.com>), which has the exclusive license for the transport of MST technology and intellectual property through the Medical University of South Carolina. Then, assuming continued stakeholder interest, MST Services conducts an extensive site assessment to determine the potential viability of an

MST program and to identify any potential barriers to program effectiveness.

Target population. MST programs focus on youths who present serious clinical problems (e.g., violence, drug abuse) and are at imminent risk of out-of-home placement. Because of the intensive nature of MST services (i.e., low therapist caseloads), the economic viability of MST programs is often predicated on reducing out-of-home placements. As such placements typically cost in the range of $20,000 to $70,000 per youth, successful MST programs are highly cost effective. Indeed, the Washington State Institute for Public Policy (1998) concluded that MST was the most effective of a wide variety of interventions designed to reduce serious criminal activity by adolescents.

Funding. An important goal in the development of more effective mental health and juvenile justice services is to shift the emphasis of funding from out-of-home placements, which currently constitutes 70% of service dollars, to evidence-based community programs. Currently, MST programs are primarily funded from three main sources of revenue: Medicaid reimbursement under family preservation or rehabilitation options; shifting of government dollars from placements to intensive community services; and making MST a component of the continua of care operated by managed care organizations. Depending on local salary structures, one MST team costs approximately $225,000 per year and has the capacity to treat 45 to 50 families.

Organizational context. MST programs are usually housed within public or private sector organizations that provide mental health services. Such settings are more likely to have a culture that emphasizes rehabilitation versus punishment for youth presenting serious problems. The success of the program, however, is dependent on strong collaboration with referral sources such as juvenile justice and the family court. MST therapists often work closely with juvenile justice and social welfare professionals to assure that the perspectives of the multiple stakeholders are incorporated into youth and family treatment goals.

Facility resources necessary. Relatively little facility space is needed because MST practitioners provide services primarily in home, school, and neighborhood settings. Therapists require cellular phones, pagers, and transportation, however.

Staffing. The typical MST program includes two or three teams of three therapists each. The therapists are usually masters level, though highly qualified bachelors level clinicians are sometimes used. Each therapist carries a caseload of four to six families, and the average duration of treatment is about 4 months. Hence, each therapist treats approximately 15 families per year. In addition, the program includes an on-site doctoral level supervisor (highly experienced master's level supervisors are sometimes included) who provides at least 25% time per MST team as the clinical supervisor. Most sites also include an individual, or at least a percentage of an individual, who functions as the program administrator.

Training of staff. Training in MST is provided on-site by MST Services using essentially the same protocol that has been used in successful clinical trials of MST. Therapists and supervisors receive 5 days of intensive orientation to MST principles and clinical procedures, booster training for 1.5 days per quarter, and ongoing case consultation by an MST expert. In addition, supervisors are trained in the MST supervisory protocol, and the MST expert devotes significant resources to building the supervisor's competency and helping him or her develop supervisees' clinical skills. The MST expert also provides organizational and community consultation as needed.

Quality assurance. As noted previously, findings from recent clinical trials with violent and chronic juvenile offenders (Henggeler et al., 1997) and substance-abusing juvenile offenders (Henggeler, Pickrel, & Brondino, 1999) as well as structural modeling research (Huey et al., in press) have shown that therapist adherence to the MST treatment protocol is associated with more favorable clinical outcomes. These established links between treatment fidelity and youth outcomes have reinforced an already strong commitment to quality assurance in MST programs. As noted previously, a set of interconnected quality assurance mechanisms is used in all MST programs to provide clinicians with the resources and clinical support needed to be successful with challenging clinical cases.

TRANSPORTABILITY

With the emerging success of the MST model, especially in reducing long-term rates of rearrest and out-of-home placement for violent and chronic juvenile offenders, Henggeler and his colleagues at the Family Services Research Center (FSRC), Medical University of South Carolina, began to receive requests for dissemination of the program from public and private provider organizations in the early 1990s. The initial response of the FSRC was to attempt to transport MST following the quality assurance protocols used in the clinical trials and employing FSRC clinical research faculty as trainers and consultants. Although a modest degree of success was achieved using this approach, two substantive sets of difficulties emerged during the first 2-3 years of dissemination. First, the research mission of the FSRC suffered as faculty time was diverted from research projects to consultation with dissemination sites. Second, dissemination sites were not receiving a consistently high level of service and technical assistance largely because the priorities of designated consultants were grant project management, writing research manuscripts, and submitting grant applications rather than consultation to distal sites.

To address these difficulties, the FSRC leadership sought advice from respected administrative leaders at the Medical University. The clear consensus was that MST dissemination efforts should be privatized, and that the newly formed dissemination group should develop an exclusive licensing agreement with the university for the transfer of MST technology and intellectual property. MST Services, Inc. was established in 1996 and developed such an agreement in collaboration with the university. At present, the decision to privatize MST dissemination efforts has been very successful. The FSRC now includes 50 faculty and staff and has a clearly focused research mission. MST Services includes eight full-time consultants and several part-time consultants. Most important, however, the mission of MST Services is clear and unambiguous–the absolute priority of the organization is to disseminate MST with fidelity and to effectively address barriers to such fidelity across therapist, supervisor, organizational, and community levels. As of November, 1999, MST programs have been transported to 20 states, Canada, and Norway, with approximately 2,000 families served annually. Moreover, the success of both the FSRC and MST Services has enabled collaboration on NIMH and Office of Juvenile Justice and Delinquency Prevention funded research on the supervisory and organizational determinants of effective MST dissemination (i.e., dissemination that maintains program fidelity, achieves client outcomes).

CLINICAL AND SERVICE OUTCOMES

More than 850 families have participated in the eight MST clinical trials that have been published. These trials included:

- 3 with violent and chronic juvenile offenders, with follow-ups ranging from 1.7 to 4.0 years (Borduin et al., 1995; Henggeler, Melton, & Smith, 1992; Henggeler, Melton, Smith, Schoenwald, & Hanley, 1993; Henggeler et al., 1997),
- 1 with youths presenting mental health emergencies (i.e., suicidal, homicidal, psychotic) (Henggeler, Rowland et al., 1999; Schoenwald, Ward, Henggeler, & Rowland, in press),
- 1 with juvenile offenders meeting DSM-III criteria for substance abuse or dependence (Brown, Henggeler, Schoenwald, Brondino, & Pickrel, 1999; Henggeler, Pickrel, & Brondino, 1999; Schoenwald, Ward, Henggeler, Pickrel, & Patel, 1996),
- 1 with a small sample of juvenile sexual offenders and a 3-year follow-up (Borduin, Henggeler, Blaske, & Stein, 1990),
- 1 with inner-city delinquents (Henggeler et al., 1986),
- 1 with maltreating families (Brunk, Henggeler, & Whelan, 1987).

Clinical outcomes. Several sets of findings have emerged consistently. In comparison with control conditions, youths in the MST condition have demonstrated significantly improved emotional and behavior functioning. For example, across several follow-ups, recidivism rates have been decreased between 25% to 70%. MST also has been particularly effective at improving family relations based on both self-report and observational measures. Such improvement is critical toward achieving reductions in behavior problems (Huey et al., in press). In addition, school attendance for MST participants has improved significantly in each of the two studies that evaluated such.

Service outcomes. Several of the randomized trials focused on youths who were at imminent risk of out-of-home placement in facilities such as residential treatment centers, boot camps, and psychiatric inpatient units. In comparison with control conditions, MST produced 47% to 64% decreases in long-term rates of days in out-of-home placements. These findings have led reviewers to conclude that MST is a highly cost effective treatment model (Aos, Phipps, Barnoski, & Lieb, 1999). For example, the average net gain for MST was $61,068 per youth in criminal justice system benefits and crime victim benefits, which contrasts with a net loss of $7,511 observed for juvenile boot camps.

Finally, recent studies with substance-abusing or dependent juvenile offenders (Henggeler, Pickrel, Brondino, & Crouch, 1996) and youths presenting psychiatric emergencies (Henggeler, Rowland et al.,

1999) have had treatment completion rates of 98% and 97%, respectively. Across the two studies, families averaged approximately 60 hours and 100 hours, respectively, of direct clinical contact with MST practitioners over a 4-month period. These findings support the capacity of MST to effectively engage youths and families traditionally considered resistant to treatment (Cunningham & Henggeler, 1999). This capacity most likely accounts for the high consumer satisfaction reported by families receiving MST services (Henggeler, Rowland et al., 1999).

REFERENCES

Aos, S., Phipps, P., Barnoski, R., & Lieb, R. (1999). *The comparative costs and benefits of programs to reduce crime: A review of national research findings with implications for Washington State, Version 3.0.* Olympia, WA: Washington State Institute for Public Policy.

Birmaher, B., Ryan, N. D., Williamson, D. E., Brent, D. A., & Kaufman, J. (1996). Childhood and adolescent depression: A review of the past 10 years. Part II. *Journal of the American Academy of Child and Adolescent Psychiatry, 35,* 1575-1583.

Borduin, C. M., Henggeler, S. W., Blaske, D. M. & Stein, R. (1990). Multisystemic treatment of adolescent sexual offenders. *International Journal of Offender Therapy and Comparative Criminology, 35,* 105-114.

Borduin, C. M., Mann, B. J., Cone, L. T., Henggeler, S. W., Fucci, B. R., Blaske, D. M., & Williams, R. A. (1995). Multisystemic treatment of serious juvenile offenders: Long-term prevention of criminality and violence. *Journal of Consulting and Clinical Psychology, 63,* 569-578.

Bronfenbrenner, U. (1979). *The ecology of human development: Experiments by design and nature.* Cambridge, MA: Harvard University Press.

Brown, T. L., Henggeler, S. W., Schoenwald, S. K., Brondino, M. J., & Pickrel, S. G. (1999). Multisystemic treatment of substance-abusing and dependent juvenile delinquents: Effects on school attendance at posttreatment and 6-month follow-up. *Children's Services: Social Policy, Research, and Practice, 2,* 81-93.

Brunk, M., Henggeler, S. W., & Whelan, J. P. (1987). A comparison of multisystemic therapy and parent training in the brief treatment of child abuse and neglect. *Journal of Consulting and Clinical Psychology, 55,* 311-318.

Cunningham, P. B., & Henggeler, S. W. (1999). Engaging multiproblem families in treatment: Lessons learned throughout the development of multisystemic therapy. *Family Process, 38,* 265-281.

Elliott, D. S. (1998). *Blueprints for violence prevention* (Series Ed.). University of Colorado, Center for the Study and Prevention of Violence. Boulder, CO: Blueprints Publications.

Henggeler, S. W. (1999a). Multisystemic therapy: An overview of clinical procedures, outcomes, and policy implications. *Child Psychology & Psychiatry Review, 4,* 2-10.

Henggeler, S. W. (1999b). Multisystemic treatment of serious clinical problems in children and adolescents. *Clinician's Research Digest, Supplemental Bulletin 21.*

Henggeler, S. W., Melton, G. B., Brondino, M. J., Scherer, D. G., & Hanley, J. H. (1997). Multisystemic therapy with violent and chronic juvenile offenders and their families: The role of treatment fidelity in successful dissemination. *Journal of Consulting and Clinical Psychology, 65,* 821-833.

Henggeler, S. W., Melton, G. B., & Smith, L. A. (1992). Family preservation using multisystemic therapy: An effective alternative to incarcerating serious juvenile offenders. *Journal of Consulting and Clinical Psychology, 60,* 953-961.

Henggeler, S. W., Melton, G. B., Smith, L. A., Schoenwald, S. K., & Hanley, J. H. (1993). Family preservation using multisystemic treatment: Long-term follow-up to a clinical trial with serious juvenile offenders. *Journal of Child and Family Studies, 2,* 283-293.

Henggeler, S. W., Pickrel, S. G., & Brondino, M. J. (1999). Multisystemic treatment of substance-abusing and dependent delinquents: Outcomes, treatment fidelity, and transportability. *Mental Health Services Research, 1,* 171-184.

Henggeler, S. W., Pickrel, S. G., Brondino, M. J., & Crouch, J. L. (1996). Eliminating (almost) treatment dropout of substance-abusing or dependent delinquents through home-based multisystemic therapy. *American Journal of Psychiatry, 153,* 427-428.

Henggeler, S. W., Rodick, J. D., Borduin, C. M., Hanson, C. L., Watson, S. M., & Urey, J. R. (1986). Multisystemic treatment of juvenile offenders: Effects on adolescent behavior and family interactions. *Developmental Psychology, 22,* 132-141.

Henggeler, S. W., Rone, L., Thomas, C., & Timmons-Mitchell, J. (1998). *Blueprints for violence prevention: Multisystemic therapy.* D. S. Elliott (Series Ed.), University of Colorado, Center for the Study and Prevention of Violence. Boulder, CO: Blueprints Publications.

Henggeler, S. W., Rowland, M. R., Randall, J., Ward, D., Pickrel, S. G., Cunningham, P. B., Miller, S. L., Edwards, J. E., Zealberg, J., Hand, L., & Santos, A. B. (1999). Home-based multisystemic therapy as an alternative to the hospitalization of youth in psychiatric crisis: Clinical outcomes. *Journal of the American Academy of Child & Adolescent Psychiatry, 38,* 1331-1339.

Henggeler, S. W., & Schoenwald, S. K. (1998). *The MST supervisory manual: Promoting quality assurance at the clinical level.* Charleston, SC: MST Institute.

Henggeler, S. W., Schoenwald, S. K., Borduin, C. M., Rowland, M. D., & Cunningham, P. B. (1998). *Multisystemic treatment of antisocial behavior in children and adolescents.* New York: Guilford Press.

Huey, S. J., Henggeler, S. W., Brondino, M. J., & Pickrel, S. G. (in press). Mechanisms of change in multisystemic therapy: Reducing delinquent behavior through therapist adherence and improved family and peer functioning. *Journal of Consulting and Clinical Psychology.*

Kazdin, A. E., & Weisz, J. R. (1998). Identifying and developing empirically supported child and adolescent treatments. *Journal of Consulting and Clinical Psychology, 66,* 19-36.

Loeber, R., & Hay, D. (1997). Key issues in the development of aggression and violence from childhood to early adulthood. *Annual Review of Psychology, 48,* 371-410.

McBride, D., VanderWaal, C., VanBuren, H., & Terry, Y. (1997). *Breaking the cycle of drug use among juvenile offenders.* Washington, DC: National Institute of Justice.

Schoenwald, S. K. (1998). *Multisystemic therapy consultation guidelines.* Charleston, SC: MST Institute.

Schoenwald, S. K., Ward, D. M., Henggeler, S. W., Pickrel, S. G., & Patel, H. (1996). MST treatment of substance-abusing or dependent adolescent offenders: Costs of reducing incarceration, inpatient, and residential placement. *Journal of Child and Family Studies, 5,* 431-444.

Schoenwald, S. K., Ward, D. M., Henggeler, S. W., & Rowland, M. D. (in press). MST vs. hospitalization for crisis stabilization of youth: Placement outcomes 4 months post-referral. *Mental Health Services Research.*

Stanton, M. D., & Shadish, W. R. (1997). Outcome, attrition, and family-couples treatment for drug abuse: A meta-analysis and review of the controlled, comparative studies. *Psychological Bulletin, 122,* 170-191.

Tate, D. C., Reppucci, N. D., & Mulvey, E. P. (1995). Violent juvenile delinquents: Treatment effectiveness and implications for future action. *American Psychologist, 50,* 777-781.

Washington State Institute for Public Policy (1998). *Watching the bottom line: Cost-effective interventions for reducing crime in Washington.* Olympia, WA: The Evergreen State College.

Community-Based Treatment
for Adjudicated Delinquents:
The Oregon Social Learning Center's
"Monitor" Multidimensional Treatment
Foster Care Program

Kevin J. Moore, PhD
Peter G. Sprengelmeyer, PhD
Patricia Chamberlain, PhD

SUMMARY. The following article outlines an empirically-validated treatment approach for addressing chronic, delinquent behavior in adolescents and their families: Multidimensional Treatment Foster Care (MTFC). MTFC grew out of evidence for the effectiveness of behavioral parent training approaches and a clinical need for programs to address the behavior of delinquent adolescents who have been found to be beyond parental control. MTFC starts with a focus on the need to return the adolescent to the family and community, and, thus, the program stresses the generalization of treatment effects. Recent replication studies are reviewed that demonstrate the effectiveness, utility, and cost-effectiveness of the MTFC program. *[Article copies available for a fee from The Haworth Document Delivery Service: 1-800-342-9678. E-mail address: <getinfo@ haworthpressinc.com> Website: <http://www.HaworthPress.com> © 2001 by The Haworth Press, Inc. All rights reserved.]*

Kevin J. Moore, PhD, Peter G. Sprengelmeyer, PhD, and Patricia Chamberlain, PhD, are all affiliated with the Oregon Social Learning Center.

[Haworth co-indexing entry note]: "Community-Based Treatment for Adjudicated Delinquents: The Oregon Social Learning Center's 'Monitor' Multidimensional Treatment Foster Care Program." Moore, Kevin J., Peter G. Sprengelmeyer, and Patricia Chamberlain. Co-published simultaneously in *Residential Treatment for Children & Youth* (The Haworth Press, Inc.) Vol. 18, No. 3, 2001, pp. 87-97; and: *Innovative Mental Health Interventions for Children: Programs That Work* (ed: Steven I. Pfeiffer, and Linda A. Reddy) The Haworth Press, Inc., 2001, pp. 87-97. Single or multiple copies of this article are available for a fee from The Haworth Document Delivery Service [1-800-342-9678, 9:00 a.m. - 5:00 p.m. (EST). E-mail address: getinfo@haworth pressinc.com].

KEYWORDS. Community intervention, adjudicated youth, treatment foster care

The Oregon Social Learning Center (OSLC) is a multidisciplinary research and development center that has focused for the last 30 years on increasing the scientific understanding of social and psychological processes related to healthy development and family functioning. Researchers at OSLC apply an understanding of human development and healthy functioning to the design and evaluation of interventions that strengthen children, adolescents, families, and communities. OSLC's Multidimensional Treatment Foster Care (MTFC) program (Chamberlain, 1994) has been developed in this unique research and development context. The following is a short history of the development of MTFC.

Initial research at OSLC and at the University of Oregon by Gerald Patterson, John B. Reid, and their colleagues (cf. Patterson, 1982) suggested that moment-by-moment contingencies within the interactions of family members explain much of the variance in child development outcomes. In addition, there was an accumulation of evidence that during adolescence peers contribute to developmental outcomes, particularly in the area of delinquency and violence (Dishion & Patterson, 1997; Patterson, Reid, & Dishion, 1992; Stoolmiller, 1994). During the late 1960s and 70s, researchers at OSLC and elsewhere (e.g., Forehand & McMahon, 1981; Wahler, 1976) developed behavioral family therapy and parent training approaches specifically targeting the interactions between parents and their behaviorally disordered children. In particular, these approaches attempted to alter a family's moment-by-moment social interactions such that coercive interchanges were disrupted through non-violent limit setting (e.g., time-out and response cost) and the use of positive contingencies for developmentally appropriate behavior. Outcome studies (Forehand & Long, 1988; Patterson, Chamberlain, & Reid, 1982) suggested that these behavioral interventions helped reduce problem behaviors with young and latency-aged children and increased positive parent-child interaction patterns.

In the late 1970s and early 80s, OSLC worked to extend these successful early childhood and latency-aged behavioral parent training/ behavioral family therapy treatments for use with adolescents. The treatments developed were generally effective when they were applied to adolescents with severe acting out behaviors and adjudicated adolescents (Bank, Marlowe, Reid, Patterson, & Weinrott, 1991). However, by the time families were referred for treatment, there was often so much chaos, out-of-control behavior, and well-established negative emotional reactions between the youth and his parents that it was difficult to teach the parents the necessary skills to effectively parent their child. In addition, OSLC's emphasis on a one-mechanism parent training intervention that targeted coercive interaction sequences was found to be necessary but not sufficient to alter the negative developmental trajectories of adolescents. It became obvious that the influence of negative peers, failure in other settings (e.g., school, work), and alienation from parents and other socializing adults were also associated with the maintenance and escalation of negative developmental trajectories.

In attempts to generalize behavioral parent training to adolescents, both treatment and research staff began to hypothesize alternatives to a single-mechanism approach to treatment. The central difficulty appeared to be the need to separate the youth and his or her parents to address concerns outside of the pressure from the ongoing, conflictual relationship. Such separation would interrupt the highly ritualized patterns of family interactions and would permit other areas implicated in severe adolescent problem behaviors (e.g., deviant dress, inability to delay gratification) to be addressed. At about this time, the State of Oregon requested proposals for proctor foster care programs that targeted 12- to 18-year-old adjudicated youths who were incarcerated and returning home, and the MTFC program was developed as a logical extension of the OSLC's parent training and behavioral family therapy treatments.

In addition to the clinical problems noted above, development of MTFC was viewed as an opportunity to begin to address a general problem with treatment models for youth who have severe behavioral and emotional modulation problems: the *generalizability of treatment effects.* Perhaps the most dramatic of society's attempts to reduce the problems of troubled youths and their families is removing youths from their homes and placing them in residential institutions. Although some of the extant research has shown that significant treatment effects are often evident while the youth is *within the institution,* after a youth leaves the institution these treatment effects typically fade (Bank, Marlowe, Reid, Patterson, & Weinrott, 1991).

Our conclusion from the outcomes of the last 40-50 years of public policy is that attempts to produce individual behavioral changes in youths and to hope that these changes generalize and effectively compete with the socializing influences of family, peers, siblings, and teachers do not work. Therefore, our approach to the problem of generalization of treatment effects from residential environments back into community-based settings and the difficulty of treating families of adjudicated delinquents was the use of a "proctor" family to "treat" the child while conjoint family therapy was also taking place. In addition to our own experiences with behavioral parent training and family therapy, our initial model of "treatment foster care" was influenced by the work of Robert Hawkins and his colleagues using a treatment foster care treatment model for children with mental health difficulties (Hawkins, Meadowcroft, Trout, & Luster, 1985).

The state's willingness to begin to develop funding sources for community and family-based treatments, such as treatment foster care, also appeared to be greatly influenced by the many parent and professional advocacy groups that were concerned with the application of treatment technologies in mental health, developmental disabilities, and special education. These parents and professionals were advocating for treatments based on the "least restrictive alternative" in terms of both treatment procedures and living environments. The MTFC program appears to meet these goals of creating a least restrictive environment that is flexible to the individual needs of the youth being served and that is similar to the environment to which the youth is supposed to generalize the learned behaviors (e.g., biological parents' home). The following sections of this chapter will discuss the services offered within the MTFC program, treatment delivery and fidelity, and outcome evaluations.

DESCRIPTION OF SERVICES

The MTFC program uses a comprehensive treatment model, including: (a) foster parent recruitment and screening, (b) intensive pre-service training, (c) ongoing foster parent consultation from professional staff, (d) school consultation, individual youth treatment, and family therapy, and (e) aftercare services using a "wraparound" or customized service delivery for the youths and their families.

Foster parent recruitment and screening. Both one- and two-parent families from diverse social, ethnic, and economic backgrounds have successfully served as MTFC foster parents. Because of the magnitude of the problems presented by the children, families who are selected must be willing to work actively, consistently, and cooperatively toward specific behavioral goals for the child placed with them. Recruitment is done primarily through word of mouth, particularly from current MTFC foster parents, who are paid a "finders fee" for referring others who become MTFC foster parents.

Pre-service training. The content and methods of the pre-service training were adapted from the clinical parent training programs and methods developed at OSLC. Therefore, MTFC foster parent training is similar to the social learning parent-training model, which has been used and replicated in treatment studies since the late 1960s. This training model requires foster parents to engage daily in specific, predetermined treatment activities for the youth placed in the home. The treatment activities are organized into a plan that focuses on teaching the youth relevant family living, social, academic, recreational, and vocational skills.

All foster parents complete the 20- to 30-hour pre-service training that covers social learning principles such as observing and identifying specific target behaviors, using effective praise, pre-teaching, setting clear and consistent limits, and using positive consequences and sanctions. The training also addresses developmental issues (including attachment, separation, and relationship development), motivational strategies, legal and ethical issues (e.g., creation of safe environments, youth rights, concerns related to prior abuse), communication and problem-solving strategies (e.g., preventing confrontations), and professional concerns (e.g., retaining perspective when working with biological families, teachers, and social welfare caseworkers).

MTFC foster parents are trained to adapt the general program principles to the specific daily teaching needs of the youth placed with them. An individualized point-and-level system (or some developmentally appropriate contingency management system such as a star chart for younger children) with daily feedback (point card) is used. The level system and daily point cards have been developed so that the foster parents and consultants can clearly specify the minimal daily expectations (e.g., getting up on time; chores; attending school; completing homework; following adult instructions). The level system and daily point cards also direct the youth toward how increased privileges and responsibilities can be earned. On a program level, the daily point card provides a structure for foster parents to reinforce and provide minor consequences to the child for moment-to-moment social interactions and behaviors. The point-and-level system is divided into three levels that gradually give the youth more privileges and responsibilities, with Level 3 moving the youth as far towards independent living as developmentally appropriate.

Ongoing foster parent consultation. Once a child is placed in an MTFC home, professional consultation is provided to the foster parent(s) in order to establish and maintain a stable placement. The foster parents are supervised in teaching and reinforcing skills that facilitate healthy and functional parent-child interactions. The youth is taught (by earning and losing points and privileges, role-plays, spontaneous teaching, and counseling) on a moment-by-moment basis those skills that have been shown to decrease parent-child conflict, disruptive child behaviors, and to improve the child's relationships with adults. Daily behaviors and activities are tracked carefully and then matched to the child's developmental and social functioning level. During this process, the child remains accountable for his behavior and emotional state and is taught to use functional social behavior in small shaping steps. The foster parents meet daily with the youth to tally points and provide feedback so that the child knows what was done well and where improvement is needed. This feedback process provides an opportunity for the foster parents to encourage positive behaviors (e.g., by giving extra points, using high rates of spontaneous praise and acknowledgment), and to discourage non-functional behaviors (e.g., giving small consequences such as loss of points, time out, privilege removal, or a small chore).

School consultation, individual counseling, and family counseling. Although the primary treatment effects from MTFC are seen as arising from the ongoing feedback the youth receives within the MTFC home regarding his behavior, the MTFC program also attempts to intervene in other systems with which the youth is involved (e.g., school consultation and interventions, individual treatments and family therapy). All such interventions are based on the same social learning principles that guide interactions between the foster parent and youth (see Chamberlain, 1994, for a more complete description of these interventions).

Aftercare. Aftercare services offered to program youths and their families are based on those services found to be helpful for the MTFC foster families. These services include 24-hour crises intervention, group and/or individual consultation and support, school consultation and intervention, individual and family therapy, backup consequences (e.g., time out at the Center, supervised work chores, talking with probation officer, receiving money for contingency contracts), money for transportation, and youth and family incentives for sustained progress.

Treatment Delivery and Fidelity

In this family-based treatment model it is the foster parents who provide most of the "treatment" for youths in the program. Our recent research (Chamberlain & Moore, 1998; Chamberlain & Reid, 1998) strongly suggests that it is the moment-to-moment contingencies and parental monitoring that shape and maintain youths' (in)appropriate behavior. Because youths who enter the MTFC program have often learned that extremes of coercive behavior can achieve desired outcomes, the foster parents working with these children need to be supported as professionals. In addition, encouraging responsible behavior from adolescents while in foster care is not the final goal of the MTFC program. The ultimate target is for the youth to return to the least restrictive environment in which their needs can be met (often this is the home of the biological parents). Therefore, program staff members support interventions in the MTFC home to assist in generalizing the youth's behavioral changes in other environments (e.g., community, school).

The MTFC model was developed with great care to ensure that the treatment was flexible enough to meet the needs of individual youths and their families (Chamberlain, 1994). At the same time, treatment fidelity is a focus of training and clinical supervision throughout the program. For example, pre-service training and weekly mandatory supervision (i.e., foster parent support groups and clinical supervision groups) are used to monitor adherence to the MTFC treatment model while addressing the current needs/strengths of youths in the program. Supervision and monitoring is also necessary to direct clinical staff and foster parents toward a coherent set of interventions and away from being reactive to isolated situations.

Another important treatment fidelity check is the use of a daily (weekdays) telephone call where data is collected (using the Parent Daily Report; Chamberlain & Reid, 1987) regarding the youth's progress/problems during the past 24 hours. The Parent Daily Report (PDR) caller also helps to monitor foster parent responses to problem behaviors and alerts staff members to potential problems. PDR data can then be used to focus supervision meetings, track treatment fidelity, and monitor behavioral change/patterns.

Replication/Outcome Evaluation Research

There are several replication projects concerning MTFC that have only recently been initiated. The MTFC program was chosen by the University of Colorado's Center for the Study and Prevention of Violence as one of ten "Blueprint" programs. "Blueprint" programs were carefully selected based on scientific evidence of effectiveness, and the program's readiness for replication beyond the founding site. Currently, MTFC is being replicated in three sites (Lynchburg, VA; Flagstaff, AZ; Allentown, PA). However, it is too early in this federally-funded dissemination effort to evaluate the success or failure of these replications. In addition to the "Blueprint" replications, a large childcare agency in Tennessee has been using the MTFC model as part of a statewide continuum of care contract. This agency has received training and ongoing clinical consultation for the past three years. Anecdotal reports from this agency suggest that using the MTFC model has reduced residential care costs, improved the placement stability, and reduced foster parent turnover.

Our experiences with disseminating this program has taught us that one of the most difficult aspects of the program to maintain is the culture of pro-active, positive treatment in the face of coping with very troubled youths and their biological families. Other unique aspects of the program that can be difficult to maintain are the emphases on the dealing with behavioral problems through positive reinforcement of replacement behaviors and addressing problems in the here-and-now with the use of contingencies. Dealing with behavior through coordinated moment-by-moment contingencies may be especially difficult for mental health agencies where staff members have been trained to work independently and use individual insight-oriented therapy or well-intentioned "talk" as the cornerstone of effective treatment. A consistent supervision relationship with a person clearly versed in the treatment approach appears to adequately address these difficult fidelity issues.

Outcome evaluations. If adequate resources were available, a multi-method/multi-agent outcome evaluation with participants randomly assigned to treatment conditions would be the optimal form for an

MTFC evaluation. However, few applied settings will have the resources to conduct such an evaluation. Thus, any planned program evaluation should attempt to use existing third party information sources (e.g., official arrest records, school records, and a validated measure of post-program living situation). Program evaluations should also look at the impact of treatment beyond the direct effects on the youth who were served. Other areas of treatment impact include retention of foster parents and community consumer satisfaction (e.g., referral sources, foster and biological parents, the youth, schools, etc.). Even without multiple evaluation sites, the beginning of a published database of MTFC outcomes does exist in the literature (e.g., Chamberlain & Moore, 1998; Chamberlain & Reid, 1998).

Chamberlain and Reid (1998) showed that compared to youths treated in group care (GC) settings, youths treated in the MTFC program were re-arrested significantly less often and were returned home to live with parents or relatives significantly more often. The relative predictive power of the treatment condition variable (i.e., GC or MTFC) compared to other predictors of future delinquent behaviors (e.g., age at first arrest, age at referral to treatment) also demonstrated several important relationships. Multiple regression analyses showed that the treatment condition (i.e., GC or MTFC) predicted both official and self-reported criminality at follow-up beyond other well-known predictors of chronic juvenile offending (i.e., age at first offense, number of previous offenses, age at referral). This positive intervention finding is remarkable given the recent work by Patterson and his colleagues (e.g., Patterson, 1996) concerning the extremely strong association between early arrest and chronic juvenile arrest rates (.50-.80). Additionally, age at referral to MTFC did not account for significant independent variance in outcomes. That is, the program was able to affect similar levels of change in older and younger delinquents. More typically, greater behavioral change can be achieved with younger children and less with adolescents (cf. Patterson, Dishion, & Chamberlain, 1993). Chamberlain and Reid's findings imply that treating even older, early-onset delinquents with strong, well-trained, and supported MTFC families has the potential to change their delinquent trajectories.

Clinical utility. In addition to the efficacy studies mentioned above, several recent reviews (American Psychological Association, 1994; Jacobson & Christensen, 1999) have suggested that even an effective intervention is of only limited clinical utility without a clear demonstration of relative cost effectiveness, generalizability, and feasibility. The feasibility of MTFC programs appears to be addressed by the multiple program implementations; additionally, both the cost effectiveness and generalizability of this treatment approach have been addressed in the extant literature.

Aos, Phipps, Barnoski, and Leib (1999) included MTFC in an independent cost-effectiveness study of interventions for juvenile offenders. For example, when societal expenses associated with juvenile offending (e.g., court costs, victim costs, property damage, and out-of-home care costs) are included in the cost-effectiveness algorithms, by the time subjects are age 25, MTFC saves taxpayers over $17,000 compared to usual services. Moreover, the analysis revealed that program costs were recaptured within two years post treatment.

The MTFC program was created to address the behavioral problems presented by delinquent adolescent males. Over the past 15 years, generalization of the MTFC model has been addressed with the application of the model to a variety of different target populations. Given that MTFC represents an out-of-home intervention approach, the target populations include only those children and adolescents who cannot be maintained in the family home. For example, MTFC has been evaluated in a randomized trial of service provision for children exiting a state mental hospital (Chamberlain & Reid, 1991). In addition, several current projects are currently underway at OSLC to apply and evaluate MTFC with adjudicated female adolescents, younger children (aged 4 to 6), and youth with borderline intellectual functioning (i.e., IQ testing results between 70-85). Initial data from these projects suggest both that the general parameters of MTFC programs are effective with a variety of different, hard-to-treat populations, and that important adjustments are necessary to optimize treatment effectiveness.

REFERENCES

American Psychological Association, Task Force on Psychological Intervention Guidelines. (1994). Washington, DC: Author.

Aos, S., Phipps, P., Barnoski, R., & Leib, R. (1999). *The comparative costs and benefits of programs to reduce crime: A review of national research findings with implications for Washington state.* Olympia, WA: Washington State Institute for Public Policy.

Bank, L., Marlowe, J. H., Reid, J. B., Patterson, G. R., & Weinrott, M. R. (1991). A comparative evaluation of parent training for families of chronic delinquents. *Journal of Abnormal Child Psychology, 19,* 15-33.

Chamberlain, P. (1994). *Family connections: Treatment Foster Care for adolescents with delinquency.* Eugene, OR: Northwest Media.

Chamberlain, P., & Moore, K. J. (1998). A clinical model for parenting juvenile offenders: A comparison of group care versus family care. *Clinical Psychology and Psychiatry, 3*(3), 375-386.

Chamberlain, P., & Reid, J. B. (1987). Parent observation and report of child symptoms. *Behavioral Assessment, 9,* 97-109.

Chamberlain, P., & Reid, J. B. (1991). Using a Specialized Foster Care community treatment model for children and adolescents leaving a state mental hospital. *Journal of Community Psychology, 19,* 266-276.

Chamberlain, P., & Reid, J. B. (1998). Comparison of two community alternatives to incarceration for chronic juvenile offenders. *Journal of Consulting and Clinical Psychology, 66*(4), 624-633.

Dishion, T., & Patterson, G. R. (1997). The timing and severity of antisocial behavior: Three hypotheses within an ecological framework. In D. M. Stoff, J. Breiling, & J. D. Maser (Eds.), *Handbook of antisocial behavior* (pp. 205-217). New York: John Wiley & Sons, Inc.

Forehand, R., & Long, N. (1988). Outpatient treatment of the acting out child: Procedures, long term follow-up data, and clinical problems. *Advances in Behaviour Research and Therapy, 10,* 129-177.

Forehand, R., & McMahon, R. (1981). Helping the noncompliant child: A clinician's guide to parent training. New York: Guilford Press.

Hawkins, R. P., Meadowcroft, P., Trout, B. A., & Luster, W. C. (1985). Foster family-based treatment. *Journal of Clinical Child Psychology, 14*(3), 220-228.

Jacobson, N. S., & Christensen, A. (1999). Studying the effectiveness of psychotherapy: How well can clinical trials do the job? *American Psychologist, 51*(10), 1031-1039.

Patterson, G. R. (1982). *A social learning approach to family intervention: III. Coercive family process.* Eugene, OR: Castalia.

Patterson, G. R. (1996). Some characteristics of a developmental theory for early-onset delinquency. In M. F. Lenzenweger & J. J. Haugaard (Eds.), *Frontiers of Developmental Psychopathology* (pp. 81-124). New York: Oxford University Press.

Patterson, G. R., Chamberlain, P., & Reid, J. B. (1982). A comparative evaluation of parent training procedures. *Behavior Therapy, 13,* 638-650.

Patterson, G. R., Dishion, T. J., & Chamberlain, P. (1993). Outcomes and methodological issues relating to treatment of antisocial children. In T. R. Giles (Ed.), *Handbook of effective psychotherapy* (pp. 43-88). New York: Plenum Press.

Patterson, G. R., Reid, J. B., & Dishion, T. J. (1992). *A social learning approach. IV. Antisocial boys.* Eugene, OR: Castalia.

Stoolmiller, M. (1994). Antisocial behavior, delinquent peer association and unsupervised wandering for boys: Growth and change from childhood to early adolescence. *Multivariate Behavioral Research, 29,* 263-288.

Wahler, R. G. (1976). Deviant child behavior within the family: Developmental speculations and behavior change strategies. In H. Leitenberg (Ed.), *Handbook of behavior modification and behavior therapy* (pp. 516-545). Englewood Cliffs, NJ: Prentice-Hall.

The Teaching-Family Model:
A Replicable System of Care

Kathryn A. Kirigin, PhD

SUMMARY. For nearly 30 years, the Teaching-Family technology of treatment, staff training, and program evaluation has been faithfully applied within diverse human service agencies throughout the country. The model serves as a means to organize and orient child care agencies and direct care providers, to provide a common ground for dealing with youngsters in residential treatment settings. The philosophy of care derives from the natural strengths of families bolstered by knowledgeable, accessible, and helpful support staff. The Teaching-Family Model was developed over a 20 year period through the collaborative efforts of NIMH, the Achievement Place Research Project at the University of Kansas, and several community-based group homes in Kansas. Within the Teaching-Family model of residential treatment for difficult youth, problem behaviors are dealt with by creating supportive family-style home environments staffed by professional teaching-parents serving 6 to 8 residents. The homes are typically affiliated with local social service agencies that provide Teaching-Family Model training, consultation, and evaluation services. Agencies providing Teaching-Family services undergo routine consumer-based and on-site evaluations, carried out by the National Teaching-Family Association to assure that treatment, training, and evaluation services are being implemented faithfully. *[Article copies available for a fee from The Haworth Document Delivery Service: 1-800-342-9678. E-mail address: <getinfo@haworthpressinc.com> Website: <http://www.HaworthPress. com> © 2001 by The Haworth Press, Inc. All rights reserved.]*

KEYWORDS. Teaching Family Model, high risk youth, residential treatment

Kathryn A. Kirigin is affiliated with the University of Kansas.

[Haworth co-indexing entry note]: "The Teaching-Family Model: A Replicable System of Care." Kirigin, Kathryn A. Co-published simultaneously in *Residential Treatment for Children & Youth* (The Haworth Press, Inc.) Vol. 18, No. 3, 2001, pp. 99-110; and: *Innovative Mental Health Interventions for Children: Programs That Work* (ed: Steven I. Pfeiffer, and Linda A. Reddy) The Haworth Press, Inc., 2001, pp. 99-110. Single or multiple copies of this article are available for a fee from The Haworth Document Delivery Service [1-800-342-9678, 9:00 a.m. - 5:00 p.m. (EST). E-mail address: getinfo@haworthpressinc.com].

MISSION

The Teaching-Family Model provides an effective and replicable out-of-home treatment environment for at-risk children and youth. It also offers a caring and natural treatment system for youth.

OBJECTIVES

- To improve the quality of residential treatment for children, youth, and dependent populations in out-of-home placements.
- To create a special class of professional caregivers who have the authority, autonomy, and ability to parent difficult children.
- To promote predictable treatment effects through skill-teaching and the development of supportive relationships between the caregivers and recipients of that care.

PROGRAM HISTORY

The Teaching-Family Model (TFM) is the outgrowth of applied behavior analysis technology (Baer, Wolf, & Risley, 1968) and data-based program development (Wolf, Kirigin, Fixsen, Blase, & Braukmann, 1995) used to create a humane, effective, replicable, youth-preferred treatment environment for adjudicated adolescents in group homes. Originally developed as an alternative to institutional confinement for delinquents and "pre-delinquents," Achievement Place for Boys, established in April of 1967 in Lawrence, Kansas, became the focal point for the development of a replicable system of care to treat problem adolescents in small, family-style settings. The development and later dissemination of the TFM treatment system evolved from a long-term collaborative research effort directed by researchers at the University of Kansas and funded by the National Institute of Mental Health Center for Studies in Crime and Delinquency from 1969 through 1987.

Today, the Teaching-Family philosophy and treatment is carried out in the context of training sites, located within human service agencies, that vary from those dealing exclusively with foster care to those that oversee a continuum of service settings including group homes, foster care homes, shelter-care, and schools. Several training sites also offer parent-training and family preservation services. The characteristics common to all Teaching-Family service agencies is their provision of skill-based education, supportive consultation, and routine evaluation services to the care-staff who live and work with the resident youth. Populations served by TFM include children and adolescents with emotional, social, and academic disabilities, and children with autism.

Since 1975, the Teaching-Family Association (TFA) has served as the professional organization for agencies implementing the TFM. The Teaching-Family Association was established to monitor the quality of TFM program implementation and to offer a professional forum for the continued development and refinement of treatment and training technology. As of 1999, 24 agencies located in sixteen states and in one Canadian province were certified as Teaching-Family sites (TFA Newsletter, May, 1999).

DEFINING CHARACTERISTICS

The Teaching-Family Model is defined by its goals, staffing patterns, treatment components, and the training and support services used to create an effective, caring residential environment for problem youth. The defining characteristics of the model are outlined in Table 1.

The TFM treatment philosophy is grounded in learning theory and the belief that many problem behaviors are exacerbated by difficult environments. Within the model context, serious problem behaviors of children and youth are dealt with by creating supportive family-style environments with no more than 8 youths, staffed by a married-couple (teaching-parent practitioners) who receive the necessary skill training, support services, and routine program evaluation to enable them to implement the treatment model.

THE TEACHING-FAMILY PRACTITIONERS

The heart of the Teaching-Family Model rests with the teaching-parents who live with the residents. The teaching-parent job description is daunting. They manage the household and the treatment program for 6 to 8 children between the ages of 10 and 18. In over 50% of the programs, teaching-parents also have children of their own who live with them in the group home environment (Graham, Graham,

TABLE 1. Defining Characteristics of the Teaching-Family Model

Program Goals
1. Humane intervention procedures
2. Effective treatment of behavior problems
3. Responsive to the program consumers
4. Replicable
5. Cost-effective

Treatment Program Environment
1. Live-in direct care staff: married couple (teaching-parents)
2. Family-style living
3. Maximum of eight residents
4. Full-time teaching-parent assistant
5. Proximity and accessibility to family, school, and community settings

Treatment Program Components
1. Skill-teaching systems (descriptive praise, preventive and corrective teaching)
2. Relationship development procedures
3. Motivation systems that emphasize personal responsibility
4. Self-government systems that empower residents with decision-making skills

Program Training and Support Services for Teaching-Parents
1. Initial 40 to 80 hour orientation and skill training workshop
2. Ongoing phone and in-home consultation on program implementation
3. Routine in-service training to promote continued skill development
4. Annual consumer evaluation of program implementation as well as the quality of training, and consultation services delivered to the teaching-parents

Kirigin, & Wolf, October, 1995). As program directors, Teaching-Parents work collaboratively with those professionals and program stakeholders, including teachers, social workers, parents, probation officers, therapists and other persons who are directly involved with their youths' lives. Although the number of stakeholders varies from youth to youth and program to program, stakeholders serve as important resources for the youths and they provide teaching-parents with feedback about youth progress and problems.

TREATMENT PROGRAM COMPONENTS

All Teaching-Family practitioners use skill teaching protocols, motivation, relationship development, and self-government/problem solving strategies modified as needed to fit the setting and client characteristics.

Skill Teaching. Teaching-interactions consist of specific behavioral steps to teach social, academic and self-care skills, and to correct problem behaviors by teaching alternative behaviors. There are three major types of teaching-interactions used in Teaching-Family programs: descriptive praise, preventive teaching, and corrective-teaching. These teaching-strategies all use clear behavioral specification, demonstration of behavior whenever possible, youth-centered rationales that emphasize the natural consequences or benefits of the skill, opportunities to practice the skill, and positive consequences in the form of praise and points for efforts to learn the skill.

Motivation. The motivation system is a token economy that provides structure and incentive for youths to learn new skills by creating tangible reinforcement as consequences for youths who have often had unrewarding experiences with adults. The motivation system is designed to emphasize point earning over point loss. For every interaction involving a loss of points, teaching-parents are expected to engage the youth in at least four interactions that involve point earning activities, usually centered around teaching and rewarding the skills needed to avoid the problem that produced the original point loss. As the youth progresses through the program, both the structure and the tangible point consequences are faded in favor of more natural social consequences and privileges.

Relationship Development. Effective teaching and parenting is enhanced through the development of mutually rewarding relationships between teaching-parents and their youths. Developing a positive relationship with each child is a labor intensive process that is grounded in the teaching activities, emphasis on behavior shaping, and the setting of clear behavioral expectations. Teaching-parents use interaction styles that demonstrate pleasantness, fairness, concern for the youth, and a commitment to problem solving over punishment.

Self-Government/Problem-Solving. The self-government system, carried out in daily family meetings, provides the youths with decision-making skills and opportunities to affect program operations. Youths learn to participate in group discussion, to give constructive criticism, to accept compliments and criticism from adults and peers, and to problem solve. The intent of this self-government system is to empower them with skills to solve their own problems within the home and outside of it.

SUPPORT SERVICES:
TEACHING-PARENT TRAINING AND MENTORING

Mastering the elements of the TFM model involves a collaborative relationship between the teaching-parents and the training staff. For the first year on the job, teaching-parents are exposed to a variety of training activities. Training begins with a preservice workshop conducted by training-site staff, many of whom are former teaching-parents or associate teaching-parents. The preservice workshop requires 40 to 80 hours of classroom instruction, typically offered over a one-to-two-week period before the couple moves into the residential setting. The workshop provides an orientation to the basic TFM treatment components with an emphasis on skill performance. The trainees read about each treatment component, discuss video-taped examples, and then practice the skills in structured skill rehearsals. In addition, teaching-parents receive instruction in learning theory, professionalism, program management, treatment planning, working with consumers, licensing requirements, and recordkeeping: areas common to all Teaching-Family programs. TFM agencies also present instruction in subjects tailored to the needs of their particular agency such as budgeting, medication management, and progress report writing.

The most challenging part of the training begins when the teaching-parents move into their designated homes and start to implement the TFM. For the first few weeks, teaching-parents may be in daily contact, by phone or in person, with their consultant. As they master the basic teaching and motivation strategies and learn to develop effective relationships with the youths, consultation focus shifts to treatment planning, problem-solving, and program refinement.

The consulting relationship is one of mentoring. A consultant's primary goal is to help the teaching-parents master the treatment approach. Consulting is a labor-intensive activity and consultants typically work with a caseload of no more than four or five couples. Consultants are skill shapers, who teach the complexities of TFM implementation using the same general TFM strategies of relationship development, skill teaching, and motivation to help their couples meet performance criteria for certification as teaching-parents. Getting a couple certified as teaching-parents generally requires about a year. Once a couple attains certification, the consultant relationship is maintained to provide on-going support, to prevent program drift and to help teaching-parents continue to refine their skills (Wolf, Braukmann, & Kirigin Ramp, 1987).

Although the role of the consultant appears to be critical in creating effective teaching-parent practitioners, it is one of the least researched aspects of the TFM. To date there are only two studies, one published (CLO study) and one unpublished dissertation (Schroeder, 1996) that have addressed the role of the consultant. For the most part, TFM sites train their consultants in much the same way they train their teaching-parent couples: with workshop instruction that emphasizes skill acquisition, followed by on-the-job mentoring by an experienced TFM consultant and routine performance evaluations.

TEACHING-PARENT CERTIFICATION

Teaching-Parents are accountable professionals. To determine how well the TFM is being implemented, twice during the first year and annually thereafter, Teaching-Parents are evaluated by their program consumers and by members of their TFM training site. Agency consumers complete brief questionnaires that ask them to rate the cooperation, communication, and effectiveness of the Teaching-Parent staff. The residents complete questionnaires about the Teaching-Parents' fairness, concern, pleasantness, and effectiveness. Training-site evaluators conduct on-site program reviews, which include a two to three hour observation in the treatment setting and individual interviews with each of the residents. Evaluators rate the teaching parents' skills in applying the treatment components, and they rate the appearance and social skills of the youths in care. Evaluators also review program records and then assess the overall quality of the treatment setting. These combined consumer and performance assessments serve as the basis for certification.

A DAY IN THE LIFE

Teaching-Families are structured households. Morning activities involve getting the kids up, fed, and ready for school. In many cases, teaching-parents also transport their kids to middle school, junior high, and high school settings and retrieve them at the end of the school day. Each resident carries a daily school note (Bailey, Wolf, &

Phillips, 1970), which allows each of their teachers to provide feedback on school performance. While their residents are in school, teaching-parents are generally available to meet with counselors, teachers, therapists, social workers, probation officers and other stakeholders who are only available during regular weekday working hours. This time can also be used to schedule personal business, family time, or rest. But more often it is used to catch up on record keeping, treatment planning, consultation and training sessions.

The busiest time of the day for teaching-parents occurs when the kids come back from school in the late afternoon continuing until the youth's bedtime. When kids return from school, teaching-parents review school performance notes, monitor homework and study time, deal with dinner preparation (often with the assistance of one or more of the youths), eat as a family, monitor after-dinner clean-up activities, and convene a family conference. After family conference, there is generally an hour or two before the youth's bedtime. This time is consumed with monitoring the youth's use of privileges, then in skill teaching or counseling sessions as occasions arise.

The treatment program is structured but also easily transportable. Teaching, motivation, relationship development, and self-government activities are not restricted to any particular time or setting. Although the majority of treatment activities are carried out within the group home, treatment can also be carried out while transporting kids, shopping at the mall, dining out in a restaurant, or anywhere. What the treatment requires, however, is skillful and dedicated teaching-parents, who can communicate effectively with youths, who are vigilant at monitoring and supervising 6 to 8 active teenagers, who are quick to reward their efforts to perform skills, and who view problem behaviors as opportunities to teach adaptive behavior that will help the youths resolve or avoid future problems. This type of skill teaching appears to be most effective when teaching-parents model the very social interactions they are trying to teach, and who interact with youths in ways that demonstrate fairness and concern for them (Solnick, Braukmann, Bedlington, Kirigin, & Wolf, 1981).

The goal of TFM treatment is to get the youths out of a residential setting and back to their natural family whenever possible. For children who have no viable family resources, the intent is to get them into a long-term, stable family home. In the early years of the Teaching-Family Model program, evaluations reported average lengths of stay of about 12 months (Kirigin, Braukmann, Atwater, & Wolf, 1982) at a cost of about $12,000 per child. Today the cost of residential treatment is considerably higher with per diem rates that exceed $70 per child in most agencies. In today's social service cost-conscious environment and managed care mentality, greater emphasis has been placed on family preservation, adoption and other less expensive placement alternatives. As a result, many TFM training sites have developed a full continuum of service settings that supplement group home treatment with other less expensive alternatives including therapeutic foster-care and home-based services to families to promote family reintegration.

DISSEMINATION

The dissemination of the Teaching-Family model has been ongoing since 1972 (see Wolf et al., 1995). Agencies interested in adopting the Teaching-Model affiliate with an existing TFA certified training site as developing sites. Over a period of two to three years, administrators, trainers, consultants, and evaluators receive instruction on the implementation of the TFM. The general criterion for achieving certification requires that the developing site demonstrates the ability to provide training, consultation, and evaluation services resulting in certified teaching-parent practitioners. Determination of the adequacy of TFM program implementation rests with the TFA Certification Committee. The certification committee conducts a consumer evaluation of services for each service level: direct care providers, trainers, consultants, evaluators and administrators. A three-member review team carries out a two to three day on-site visit to review agency records, to interview staff and to visit a sample of programs.

All certified TFA training sites submit annual reports that describe their training, consultation, and evaluation activities. These reports include consumer evaluations of direct child care staff, as well as evaluations of the site's training, consultation and evaluation services. On-site reviews of each training site are carried out once every three years. Given the rigorous, labor-intensive nature of the process, it is not surprising that the number of certified training sites has remained at about 25 agencies for the past 10 years.

PROGRAM EVALUATION

The history of the data-based program development of the TFM is described in detail in Wolf et al., 1995. TFM treatment components have been evaluated using single-subject research design methods to determine effective, youth-preferred procedures. Research on staff training includes several studies demonstrating the effectiveness of the preservice workshop skill training (Braukmann, Kirigin Ramp, Tigner, & Wolf, 1984). There have been published comparative outcome evaluation studies on program effectiveness of the TFM programs in Kansas (Braukmann, Kirigin Ramp, & Wolf, 1985; Kirigin et al., 1982; Phillips, Phillips, Fixsen, & Wolf, 1974) and one comparative follow-up study of the Boys Town Family Home program based on the TFM (Larzelere, Daly, & Criste, 1998). These studies have shown consistent during-treatment effects favoring youths in Teaching-Family programs compared to youths experiencing other non-Teaching-Family residential treatment. However, the major differences between the groups, with the possible exception of social skill performance (Ramp, Gibson, & Wolf, 1990) dissipate during the first year following release from the treatment program (Kirigin et al., 1982, Braukmann et al., 1985). A later follow-up of a sample of Teaching-Family group home participants as young adults (average age of 21), showed no differences in the percent arrested for a non-traffic offense. Despite the lack of measured differences in types or rates of offending as adults, the Teaching-Family participants were more likely to receive probation, which suggests a possible enduring effect of the social skill training (Ramp et al., 1990). Though disappointing, the follow-up results are consistent with findings from nearly every delinquency prevention and intervention program that has been subjected to careful evaluation to date. There are no "easy cures" or "quick fixes" for serious problem behaviors of children and youth and their families. What the Teaching-Family Model has achieved, however, is replicability of during-treatment effectiveness–a rare accomplishment in human services.

Although the Teaching-Family Model is unique in its replicability, dissemination of the complete system to a new or existing agency is a long-term process. Training administrators, staff trainers, consultants, evaluators, and the teaching-parent staff is a daunting and labor-intensive exercise that may take 3 to 5 years to achieve. As a result, dissemination has been gradual. Using site certification and Teaching-Family newsletters to track Teaching-Family Model adoption, it appears that once certified, the Teaching-Family Sites appear to be fairly durable. Of the original six training sites certified in the 1970s, two are no longer operating and one is no longer affiliated with the Teaching-Family Association. Of the 11 sites added in the 1980s, two closed and five are no longer affiliated with TFA. Of the 16 sites added in the 1990s, all continue to operate as TFA sites.

What binds the Teaching-Family organization together is its collective commitment to excellence in treating troubled children and youth. While quick fixes and long-term cures remain elusive in the treatment of difficult children, the model provides an interim means to create positive, caring and effective environments that are valued by the consumers.

REFERENCES

Baer, D. M., Wolf, M. M., & Risley, T. R. (1968). Some current dimensions of applied behavior analysis. *Journal of Applied Behavior Analysis, 1*(1), 91-97.

Braukmann, C. J., Kirigin Ramp, K., & Wolf, M. M. (1985). Follow-up of group home youths into young adulthood (Progress Rep, Grant MH20030, to the National Institute of Mental Health). Lawrence, KS: University of Kansas, Achievement Place Research Project.

Braukmann, C. J., Kirigin Ramp, K. A., Tigner, D. M., & Wolf, M. M. (1984). The Teaching-Family approach to training group home parents: Training procedures, validation research, and outcome findings. In R. Dangle & R. Polster (Eds.), *Behavioral parent training: Issues in research and practice.* New York: Guilford Press.

Graham, B. A., Graham, G. G., Kirigin, K. A., & Wolf, M. M. (October, 1995). *Findings of a national survey of teaching-parents: Job satisfaction and burnout.* Paper presented at the Teaching-Family Association Meeting, Banff, Alberta, Canada.

Harchik, A.E., Sherman, J.A., Sheldon, J.B., & Strouse, M.C. (1992). Ongoing consultation as a method of improving performance of staff members in a group home. *Journal of Applied Behavior Analysis, 25*(3), 599-610.

Kirigin, K. A., Braukmann, C. J., Atwater, J. D., & Wolf, M. M. (1982). An evaluation of Teaching-Family (Achievement Place) group homes for juvenile offenders. *Journal of Applied Behavior Analysis, 15*, 1-16.

Larzelere, R. E., Daly, D. L., & Criste, T. R. (1998). *The follow-up evaluation of children after out-of-home placement.* Paper presented at the American Association of Children's Residential Centers, Sanibel Island, FL.

Phillips, E. L., Phillips, E. A., Fixsen, D. L., & Wolf, M. M. (1974). *The teaching-family handbook (2nd edition).* Lawrence, KS: University of Kansas Printing Service.

Ramp, K. K., Gibson, D. M., & Wolf, M. M. (1990). *The long term effects of Teaching-Family model group home treatment.* Paper presented at the Annual meeting of the National Teaching-Family Association, Snowbird, UT.

Schroeder, C.M. (1996). Consultant roles in Teaching-Family group homes. *Dissertation Abstracts International Section A: Humanities and Social Sciences.* Dec., Vol 57 (6-A)2279.

Solnick, J. V., Braukmann, C. J., Bedlington, M. M., Kirigin, K. A., & Wolf, M. M. (1981). Parent-youth interaction and delinquency in group homes. *Journal of Abnormal Child Psychology, 9,* 107-119.

Teaching-Family Newsletter (May, 1999). National Teaching-Family Association, Snowbird, UT.

Wolf, M. M., Braukmann, C. J., & Kirigin Ramp, K. A. (1987). Serious delinquent behavior as part of a significantly handicapping condition: Cures and supportive environments. *Journal of Applied Behavior Analysis, 20,* 347-359.

Wolf, M. M., Kirigin, K. A., Fixsen, D. L., Blase, K. A., & Braukmann, C. J. (1995). The Teaching-Family Model: A case study in data-based program development and refinement (and dragon wrestling). *Journal of Organizational Behavior Management, 15*(1/2), 11-68.

Index